MORE CRYPTIC PRAISE FOR
THE DICK CHENEY CODE

AHIL ARIO USBO OKBR ILLI ANTA
COMI CMAS TERP IECE
—*National Cryptographic*

"O, greet a lulu! Moral: Let's revel! Clever! Stellar!
Om! Ululate, ergo!"
—*Modern Palindrome*

"*The Dick Cheney Code* is to literature as: (a) author: genius;
(b) laugh: riot; (c) inspired: satire; (d) surefire: bestseller;
(e) Sistine Chapel: art."
—*Multiple Choice Weekly*

"We giggled, cackled, chuckled, chortled, and snickered!"
—*Onomatopoetic Quarterly*

GR8! A2RDE4CE!
—*Vanity Plate Fair*

"You, you gotta buy this friggin' book, Tony.
I'm telling you, it'll kill you, just like we killed Paulie.
You'll die laughing."
—*The Wiretappers Transcript*

T0113420

"Better than anything I read in my entire previous life!
I only wish I will have written it!"
—*Reincarnation Today*

"Eerie shrieks of laughter. . . . A pair of disembodied
hands applauds loudly. . . ."
—*Spirit World*

"There is cause for celebration. Multitudes are seized
with mirth. The evil ruler and his minions are dejected."
—*Tarot Topics*

"Wud uzb thub funnuzzzzt buksssst Ieeee everrrb
reddzznnffft."
—*Public Address Gazette*

"

"

—*Invisible Inklings*

OTHER PARODIES BY HENRY BEARD

Bored of the Rings
(with Douglas Kenney)

Poetry for Cats

The Book of Sequels
(with Christopher Cerf, Sarah Durkee, and Sean Kelly)

The No-Sweat Aptitude Test

The Official Exceptions to the Rules of Golf

The Pentagon Catalog
(with Christopher Cerf)

The Stupid Little Golf Book
(with Leslie Nielsen)

The Unshredded Files of Bill and Hillary Clinton
(with John Boswell)

The Way Things Really Work
(with Ron Barrett)

THE
DICK CHENEY CODE

A Parody

HENRY BEARD

Simon & Schuster Paperbacks

NEW YORK   LONDON   TORONTO   SYDNEY

SIMON & SCHUSTER PAPERBACKS
Rockefeller Center
1230 Avenue of the Americas
New York, NY 10020

First Simon & Schuster Paperback edition 2004

SIMON & SCHUSTER and colophon are registered trademarks
of Simon & Schuster, Inc.

For information about special discounts for bulk purchases,
please contact Simon & Schuster Special Sales at
1-800-456-6798 or business@simonandschuster.com

Designed by Julie Schroeder

Rebus drawing on page 37 by Bruce McCall

Manufactured in the United States of America

1   3   5   7   9   10   8   6   4   2

Library of Congress Cataloging-in-Publication Data is available.

ISBN-13: 978-0-7432-7002-1

THE

DICK
CHENEY
CODE

Sort of True, Semi-Actual, Quasi-Historical, Honest-to-Pretty-Goodness Facts:

THE KNIGHTS TEMPLAR were a medieval brotherhood that traced its origins to a group of crusaders who occupied a castle in Jerusalem. They prospered for two hundred years—from 1118 until their dissolution in 1318—and during that time they amassed enormous wealth and became the bankers for the French kings. Although their last Master was burned at the stake, it is rumored that a core group, the Knights Bursar (sometimes also known as the Simoleons or the Knights of Mazuma) managed to survive. Interestingly, the original name lives on as a division of Freemasonry, a worldwide semi-secret fraternal organization whose roots go back to the eighteenth century.

1

Many of the founding fathers, including George Washington, Benjamin Franklin, Chief Justice John Marshall, and John Hancock were Masons, as were Paul Revere, John Paul Jones, the Marquis de Lafayette, most of the top officers of the Continental Army, and thirteen U.S. presidents. Among the noteworthy modern-day Masons are a number of contemporary members of Congress and a popular brand of glass storage jars.

Founded in 1832, Skull and Bones is the most exclusive and mysterious of Yale's secret societies. Widely suspected of encouraging satanic practices and devil worship in its bizarre tomb-like headquarters building in New Haven, it numbers among its initiates W. Averell Harriman, Henry Luce, McGeorge Bundy, William F. Buckley, President George W. Bush and his father, President George H. W. Bush, and Senator John Kerry, as well as scores of wealthy and influential figures in media, finance, government, and academia. Undergraduate members are known as *Knights*; graduates are referred to as *Patriarchs*. Although not a Bonesman himself, Vice President Dick Cheney attended Yale. He did not graduate, but he often returns for reunions.

* * *

Even the most cursory examination of the ponderous directory universally referred to by scholars as *The White Pages* reveals beyond any doubt that every single resident of the city of Washington, DC, belongs to a venerable, arbitrary, and tyrannical organization dating to ancient Roman times that is known simply as "The Alphabetical Order."

PROLOGUE

Smithsonian Museum, The Mall, Washington, DC
11:11 PM

HEMMINGS DUMONT, the little known but widely respected Custodian of Documents, Artifacts, Memorabilia, and Historically Significant Odds and Ends at the National Museum of American History, strained against the bonds that secured him to the frame of an antique Duncan Phyfe sidechair. As he struggled to free himself from the ugly rep-stripe ties knotted tightly around his wrists and ankles, he knew he couldn't take much more punishment.

The leader of the diabolical glee club played a middle C on his surprisingly long pitch pipe, and the three other portly white men in tuxedos who filled out the quartet launched into their third rendition of "Kumbaya." They had already performed "The Old Ark's a-Moverin," "Sixteen Tons," "Hey, Mr. Tallyman, Tally Me Bananas," "Yellow Bird," "Michael, Row the Boat Ashore," "Puff, the Magic Dragon," and, of course, the Whiffenpoof Song.

"Stop, stop," Dumont pleaded. "I can't take it anymore. I'll tell you what you want to know."

The lie he was about to repeat had been agreed upon among the Keepers many decades ago. He summoned up all the completely spurious sincerity he had developed over a lifetime as an African-American academic trying to survive in a deeply racist society.

"The dog ate it," he said finally, shaking his head in feigned regret. He would have wiped a tear from his eye if he could have raised his hand.

The Pitch permitted himself a pompous little smirk. "Ah, yes," he said, his strangely singsong voice dripping with self-satisfaction. "Your answer agrees perfectly with the information we persuaded the others to provide us."

Dumont nodded wearily. He had expected this. *Of course, these honkies would have found the others—that was the whole point of this rope-a-dope.*

What he did not expect was the poisoned dart that the Pitch blew with terrible accuracy into the side of his throat using a quick, sharp puff of air from his strange flute-like pipe to propel the deadly missile. *A blowgun. I should have figured a WASP would sting.*

As the four evil crooners walked swiftly away, Dumont could feel the toxin beginning to spread through his system. He prayed he would live long enough to do what he had to do.

With superhuman effort, he raised his left arm, and with a sudden ripping sound the tie split at the seam. At the point where the neckwear had torn, he noticed a small tag: MADE IN CHINA. He smiled ruefully. *Cheap bastards—serves them right.*

As he quickly freed himself from the remaining restraints and rose unsteadily to his feet, he could feel his muscles begin to stiffen.

He knew he had very little time left. He would have to use it wisely.

CHAPTER 1

WILLIAM FRANKLIN watched the hotel television with the eye of a dedicated researcher long attuned to the fascinating possibilities of early twenty-first-century American filmmaking. The surprisingly large-busted heroines of *Project Hot Bod: Bimbos of the Kyoto Protocol* had reacted to the threat of global warming with laudable ingenuity by removing their bikini tops and joining the hunky surfers in an impressive effort to construct a formidable array of sandcastles as a first line of defense against the rising sea level. Judging by the bulges in the dudes' Speedos, some additional hard information regarding the unforeseen consequences of widespread climatological change would be emerging shortly.

The bedside telephone rang with an insistent purr. Franklin looked at his counterfeit Rolex with annoyance. It was 1:30 AM, give or take half an hour. *Probably a wrong number. Why do publishers always stick me in these cheesy chain hotels?*

Franklin paused the videotape and grabbed the handset. "Yes?"

"Professor Franklin," said a chirpy voice, "this is Todd at the front desk. There are some, uh, policemen here looking for you."

Franklin instinctively punched the rewind button and switched the channel to PBS. When you are Professor of American Popular History, Urban Mythology, and Supermarket Tabloid Science at Howard Hughes College in Rancho Melanoma, California, as well as Director of the Harding Institute of Paranoid Studies and Chairman of the Tricoastal Center for Lowbrow Culture, Folklore, and Taproom Wagers, a sense of the dignity of one's position requires constant attention to appearances.

"There must be some mistake," said Franklin. "I had merely inquired of the young lady in your handsomely appointed cocktail lounge if she would like to join me in a simple experiment I am conducting for a paper to be entitled 'Casual Intergender Social Interaction in Hotel Cocktail Lounges on Business Trips'—no harm intended."

The voice on the phone changed. "Professor, this is Agent Dan Fine of the Department of Homeland Security. We need your immediate assistance in a matter of the utmost urgency."

"Agent Fine," Franklin stammered, "there must be some mistake. I'm just a college professor."

"You can come right down, or we can come up," said Fine in a tone that Franklin remembered from the drill sergeants in his basic training unit at Fort Dix, where for some unknown reason he had been selected to receive special training in Chemical, Biological, and Radiological Warfare. Strange that he would recall that odd fact at this particular moment, but then he did hold a degree in Explanatory Dialogue and Story Advancement from UCLA.

Franklin looked around the room at some of the materials he had been examining for his paper on Sexually Stimulating Miscellanea. The life-size bimbo doll was not going to be easy to deflate.

"I'll be right down," he said.

The Georgetown Ambassador Suites Hotel had a tacky if grandiose lobby designed to hold long lines of people waiting to check in behind zigzagging rows of velvet ropes. At this hour of the morning, it was deserted, save for the slightly incongruous sight of four uniformed agents of the Transportation Security Agency setting up what looked like a typical airport screening barrier, complete with walk-through metal detector, carry-on-luggage X-ray device, collapsible metal picnic tables with a stack of large square gray rubber trays, and a couple of folding chairs.

Two classic government-issue agents in plain clothes stepped forward. "Dan Fine," said the taller of the pair. He showed a badge. "FBI, now with Homeland Security." He held out a hand, which Franklin shook gingerly.

His partner produced a large automatic pistol, aimed it to one side, and pulled the trigger. A short, cigarette-lighter-sized flame shot out of the muzzle and a combination bottle opener and corkscrew sprang out of the butt with a loud click. "Jim Dandy, Alcohol, Tobacco, and Firearms," he said.

"I'm William Franklin. Can you tell me what this is all about?"

"We'll get to that later," said Fine, motioning Franklin toward the security line. One of the uniformed agents held out a tray. "Laptop, cell phone, electronic devices? Jewelry, keys, coins, metal objects, gimmicks, plot devices?"

Dazed, Franklin emptied his pockets, took off his jacket, and put everything into the container.

"Shoes?" he asked.

"Up to you, sir," said the bored inspector.

Franklin took off his shoes and stepped through the metal detector. It chimed loudly. "Ring?" said the inspector accusingly as he gave Franklin a thorough wanding.

Franklin looked sheepishly at the heavy gold colonial-era signet ring on the third finger of his right hand. He'd worn the Franklin family heirloom for so long, he always forgot to remove it. For the umpteenth time, he examined the intaglio image of a printer's devil composed of cleverly aligned punctuation marks from an old letterpress. Two hundred years before the Internet, an ingenious ancestor of his had created the first emoticon:

$$\underset{<}{\overset{<}{}} :)$$

"Have you accepted any gifts from strangers? Were your possessions in your possession at all times? What is the purpose of your visit?"

"No, yes, I don't know," said Franklin, collecting his things.

"Okay, he's clean," said Fine. He looked at Franklin

pointedly. "We've gone to Threat Level Purple—we don't plan to take any chances."

"You know, I think it's more of a magenta or a lavender color," said Agent Dandy.

"Well, you might be right, Jim," said Fine. "I've certainly always seen some lilac, even mauve, in there. Not a full fuchsia, mind you, but a lot less blue."

As the security team dismantled the portable inspection apparatus, Fine steered Franklin out the front door. At the curb sat an anonymous-looking black Ford festooned with crepe paper. Cans and shoes were tied to the rear bumper with string, and large soaped-on letters read JUST MARRIED.

"We're doing our part to support the President's Marriage Initiative," said Fine. He motioned Franklin to take a seat in back, got behind the wheel, and turned on a dashboard-mounted police warning light. Agent Dandy climbed in the passenger side, and they headed east down M Street at high speed.

CHAPTER 2

DEXTER "COOKIE" TOLLHOUSE, '59, known at Skull and Bones as "Windpipes" D.157, settled back into the deep leather club chair, smoking a long cigar and sipping brandy from a colossal snifter.

Like all Ivy League college clubs, the Yale Club had cooperative agreements for reciprocal privileges in cities throughout North America and Europe, and Tollhouse had been welcomed to the elegant Sachem Club on Dupont Circle as warmly as any regular member. The quiet, efficient, and deferential Negro servant reminded him of the loyal retainers at the Tomb, the wonderful old colored caddies and waiters at Augusta National, and the terrific staff of black mammies at the annual Bohemian Grove blowouts.

Merritt Parkway IV, Newell Banister, and Sterling Forest had gone to bed; age seemed to have slowed them down to an extent that always surprised and, in a way, disappointed Dexter. But, of course, although they had been good solid Whiffenpoofs back at Yale—and had graduated to become tried-and-true Deathenpoofs—they weren't Bonesmen. It showed.

Tollhouse fingered the small gold pin on his watch fob. Fabricated by Tiffany, it was in the shape of a skull and crossbones with the enigmatic number 322 centered at the intersection of the two tibias.

He took a slim cell phone out of his pocket and punched a number. He hated the things and felt a stab of shame at using one here—it was strictly against club rules—but it was late, and the public rooms were empty.

After two rings, a voice spoke from the tiny handset. "Ooga-booga?"

"Boola-boola," Tollhouse responded.

"Hubba-hubba!" came the gratified reply.

Tollhouse smiled, pressed the "End" button, and pocketed the phone. With a surprisingly powerful puff, he blew a perfect smoke ring nearly thirty feet across the room, then propelled a second, smaller one directly through the hole in its center.

The Senior Patriarch will be pleased. Our little world will be secure, our secrets will be safe.

Louis Moon, the Sachem Club's longest-serving attendant, peered discreetly into the smoking room. Thirty-eight years of honorable service to the hundreds of patronizing, brain-dead ofay dickheads who belonged to the capital's most exclusive social institution had not gone unrewarded. Acting with a stunning degree of financial savvy based on a profound if unrecognized intellect, he had parlayed dozens of overheard stock tips into a fortune of nearly $6 million, much of which had gone to sustain the work of the Keepers.

Still, he felt a certain foreboding. Tollhouse wore the Devil's Pin. He was the Enemy. He would have to be watched. Someday, Moon might even have to do something more serious than spit in his brandy.

CHAPTER 3

FRANKLIN FUMBLED FOR his seat belt as the government Ford turned onto Pennsylvania Avenue, navigating through Washington's odd Masonic pattern of diagonal avenues, circles, and squares. He felt as if he were in a bad dream or, worse still, one of those dumb thrillers you buy at the airport where an ordinary guy lands in the middle of some bizarre conspiracy.

Fine seemed to read his mind. "You're probably feeling like a guy in one of those dumb thrillers you buy at the airport who's landed in the middle of some bizarre conspiracy."

"I think I deserve an explanation, or at least some

needlessly complex narrative exposition, no matter how improbable," said Franklin angrily. "Look, what the hell is going on?"

"Hey, pal, that's not the way it works around here," said Agent Dandy, turning in his seat to face Franklin. "First we give the answers—then you ask the questions."

"This unique museum, often called the 'nation's attic,' is the repository for more than sixteen million pieces of Americana, ranging from the Star-Spangled Banner and a Model T Ford to Michael Jordan's jersey and Archie Bunker's chair from *All in the Family*," said Fine.

"What is the Smithsonian?"

Dandy nodded. "This distinguished African-American scholar was the senior Custodian of Documents, Archives, Memorabilia, and Historically Significant Odds and Ends at the Smithsonian."

"Who is Hemmings Dumont?" said Franklin immediately, remembering the erudite black man who had taken him into the vaults to show him Monica Lewinsky's blue dress, Jimmy Carter's collection of dirty French postcards, and the original handwritten first draft of Nixon's enemies list.

He'd first met Dumont several years earlier when he'd helped his alma mater, the University of Pennsylvania, arrange a permanent loan to the Smithsonian of the papers of his namesake and distant forebear, William Franklin, Benjamin Franklin's talented but eccentric illegitimate son. Dumont had been tickled by the screwball inventor's dizzy gizmos, like the Paul Revere pewter dribble mug, the Waltz Hoop, the inflatable "farting" pew cushion, and the flintlock pistol that shot out a little flag at the end of a stick with YE BANG written on it. Franklin also remembered that Dumont had suddenly turned serious when he had seen a set of plans for a patented Devil Detector.

Dandy handed Franklin a large glossy black-and-white photo. "This photograph of the dead body of Mr. Dumont is evidence of a crime."

"Murdered!" said Franklin.

"No, you're supposed to say, 'What is murder?'"

Dandy passed back an ad torn from yesterday's *Washington Post*. "This man's name in a newspaper advertisement was circled by Mr. Dumont before he died."

The half-page ad announced a book signing at 8 PM at the Barnes & Noble store in Georgetown. The name marked with a heavy black felt-tip pen was that of the noted popular historian William Franklin.

"Who is me?" said Franklin tentatively, his voice cracking.

"Bingo," said Fine. "You hit the Daily Double."

---

* * *

Franklin shook his head in disbelief. Just a few short hours ago, he'd been doing his usual dog, hellhound, and pony show, answering questions from the typical wingnuts who always showed up for these things.

Well, he had to admit that when you write books like *The Medici Cipher, The Rosicrucian Cryptogram, The Nostradamus Conundrum, The Soros Palindrome,* and *The Kennedy Doublecrostic,* you have to expect a fairly exotic readership, but did they all have to ask if the entire world is run by a secret cabal led by David Rockefeller, Henry Kissinger, Queen Elizabeth, Alan Greenspan, Rupert Murdoch, and the gnomes of Zurich?

There had been one interesting query—posed by a crackpot, of course, but at least it was unusual.

"Is the Skull and Bones secret society at Yale that President Bush and his father belong to the successor to the Secarii and the Knights Templar?" Oddly, as soon as the words were spoken, a well-dressed, WASPy-looking banker type sitting in the back row of folding wooden seats immediately got up and departed.

So, it is true—if someone mentions the name of that mysterious college brotherhood, any Bonesman in the room has to immediately leave the premises.

Franklin had replied to the question with the answer any tenured lecturer would give if he wanted someday to get a cushy fellowship at Yale, or any other Ivy League college, for that matter. "There is absolutely no evidence of that connection," he said. The questioner sat down grumpily.

Technically, that was correct—there was no hard evidence. But there were plenty of rumors, including an ancient and surprisingly persistent legend that held that the thirty pieces of silver paid to Judas Iscariot for betraying Christ were recovered by a member of the secret fanatical anti-Roman group called the Secarii, or "Murderers" (the name Iscariot itself was a corruption of the Latin word *Secarius*).

These coins were held to be imbued with a demonic power, bringing instant and immense riches to whoever possessed them. If the Knights Templar did recover them during their sojourn in Jerusalem in the course of the Crusades—and their castle was in fact located at the foot of the hill called Gethsemane—it just might explain how they came to control one of the medieval world's greatest fortunes.

What had happened to that fortune was a mystery. Another mystery, shared with Franklin late last year by a tipsy professor of the History of Economics at Stanford after a half-dozen margaritas, was exactly where and how an amount of silver bullion equal in value in today's currency to a quarter of a billion dollars ended up being transferred from France to an obscure banking institution in New Haven, Connecticut, in 1778.

CHAPTER 4

AS AIR FORCE TWO banked gently to the south after take-off from Keesler Air Force Base in Biloxi, Vice President Dick Cheney gazed out of the window of the specially equipped Gulfstream V jet at the distant midnight glow of the New Orleans skyline and, farther away, in the Gulf of Mexico, the glittering lights of the sweeping manmade archipelago of offshore oil rigs scattered across the flat moonlit waters.

At the very edge of the horizon, he could just barely make out the telltale yellowish flame at the top of the flare tower of Exxon Pascagoula 4, the hulking deep-sea drilling platform that had been his Undisclosed Location for the past few weeks.

In many ways, it was his favorite secure site. The living quarters were surprisingly spacious, and though somewhat spartan, they had all the comforts the visiting oil company executives for whom they had originally been built would expect: a 600-channel, wide-screen plasma satellite television, a private exercise room, a generously stocked bar, a library of CDs and DVDs, a compact but well-equipped office, even a billiards table.

The food was excellent—roughnecks always ate well— the communications facilities were first class, and since the only way on or off the platform was by helicopter, the privacy was second to none.

To be sure, there were fancier and more exotic accommodations at the vice president's disposal. Cheney's lips formed his trademark lopsided smile as he remembered some of the amazing lairs he had called home during the previous three years: the secret suite of rooms carved out of solid granite behind the forehead of the monumental likeness of President Theodore Roosevelt at Mount Rushmore; the elegant twenty-room apartment on the thirteenth floor of an exclusive pre-war Park Avenue co-op that supposedly had no thirteenth floor; or the compact but luxurious cabin on the Goodyear blimp that cruised the skies, in plain sight, day after day, often with the added bonus of unparalleled views of major sporting events.

But no matter how splendid or unusual they were, none of the other retreats had the one thing the big metal island off the coast of Mississippi had, the one thing Cheney loved more than anything else: the smell of oil.

The pungent sulfur tang of raw crude. The sweet reek of burnt-off methane. The low, pulsing sound of the very lifeblood of the earth being pumped up from the unfathomable depths. The feeling of the elemental power of petroleum, the boundless energy locked in the hot and hidden dark places of the earth. There was nothing like it.

As the plane leveled off on a heading for Washington, Cheney glanced at his watch. Even with the time difference, they'd be at Andrews Air Force Base in plenty of time to get to the White House for the 9 AM political review. The Brat hated people to be late. Well, humor the little jerk. Cheney had been playing Hobbes the wise tiger to Bush's Calvin for so long, it was second nature by now.

The brusque but businesslike steward appeared in the aisle and handed the vice president a menu. "This evening we're serving fillet of beef or spinach lasagna with basil-chervil chicken fingers. We do regret if owing to a previous selection, the entrée of your choice is unavailable."

"I'll have the fillet," said Cheney.

The steward looked at his notepad and frowned. "I'm sorry, sir, but all we have left is the lasagna."

Cheney shrugged.

"And your beverage preference?"

"Stoli on the rocks," said Cheney.

"We have Popov, Ustinov, and Chechenaya."

Cheney rolled his eyes. There was a big difference between Air Force One and Air Force Two, and they never let you forget it. Cheney could care less. They could have the trappings, he had the power.

"What's the movie?"

"*Spy Kids, Part 2*," said the steward, passing Cheney a copy of the previous day's *Washington Post* that was missing the sports section and had the crossword puzzle already filled out.

After the steward departed, Cheney lowered his tray table and extracted a pair of folders from his briefcase. The first one was marked "Campaign Strategy Meeting." He riffled quickly through the contents. There were a half-dozen computer-manipulated intimate photographs of John Kerry with Jane Fonda, Barbra Streisand, the entire cast of *Queer Eye for the Straight Guy*, Dolly the cloned sheep, and a pound of chicken liver. There was also a painstakingly fabricated Vietnam-era Fitness Report for

Lt. John Kerry, citing him for using a two-year-old baby as a human shield during an unauthorized amphibious assault on a monastery housing young Buddhist nuns during which he beat a blind leper to death with his own crutches, and a forged application for admission to the Masters of Dcccit program of the class of 1969 at the Leningrad Institute of Subversive Studies.

In a separate envelope with the words "October Surprise" penciled on the top was a handful of glossy full-figure and close-up snapshots of the owner of a limousine service in Brooklyn who was an absolute dead ringer for Osama bin Laden. He'd been found by the same astonishingly resourceful private investigator who had stumbled on the second-generation Iraqi appliance salesman in Dearborn, Michigan, who was now earning a tidy nest egg as Saddam Hussein. Pity he'd never live to spend it.

He put aside the first folder and opened the second. It was labeled "Operation Limp Chink." Cheney smiled his wry smile. Inside was a brilliant ten-thousand-word memorandum written by Robert Bork on the doctrine of Executive Necessity, arguing that in times of imminent and overriding crisis, the only way a president could effectively fulfill his oath to protect and defend the Constitution was, in his catchy phrase, "to selectively suspend it."

Richard Perle was responsible for the wacky name.

The man was a card. The Inner Working Group had been having a protracted discussion about President Bush's steadily sinking poll numbers and the alarming erosion of support for his policies in every one of the key swing states, and Cheney had posed a hypothetical question.

Suppose we decide we don't want to have an election?

Perle had put the tips of his forefingers in the corners of his eyes and tugged them into comical Asiatic slits.

"Velly simple," he said in a stagey Chinese-waiter singsong. "No takee Viagla."

CHAPTER 5

AGENT FINE BROUGHT the government sedan to a stop on Constitution Avenue in front of the National Museum of American History, parking it behind a long line of DC police cruisers and unmarked cars from the Federal Protective Service.

Impressive as the austere, modernistic three-story marble edifice was, it represented only a small part of the extensive eight-museum Smithsonian complex that dominated the Mall with an imposing phalanx of world-class institutions celebrating the artistic, cultural, and technological achievements of a mighty nation.

Agent Dandy opened the car's rear door, and Franklin

stepped out. He looked back at the dense paragraph of purple prose and shook his head tiredly. *Who writes this stuff?*

Franklin was escorted up the curving ramp and in through the front entrance, where several Homeland Security officers were manning a long, low machine just inside the door. Fine showed his badge to one of the officers, who inspected it closely. "OK, Agent Fine, but we've been ordered to run a voice recognition check on everyone—no exceptions."

Fine nodded, stepped up to the screening device, and spoke into a microphone.

"You dirty rat," he said, doing a respectable Cagney imitation.

After a brief pause, a tinny speaker said, "Identity confirmed."

Dandy stepped up and did a pretty fair John Wayne, but he chose an obscure scrap of dialogue from *The Searchers,* and it took a moment for the clearance to go through.

Franklin took his turn at the mike. "It was a woman that drove me to drink—never stopped to thank her," he said in stagey nasal voice.

"Cary Grant?" Agent Fine ventured.

"Sounded more like Rodney Dangerfield," said Dandy.

"W. C. Fields!" said Franklin. "Come on, it's perfect."

"Impression rejected: no known match," barked the machine.

"We'll have to do a background check," said Fine.

He led Franklin to a credit card swipe slot at the end of the voice scanner. "Major cards only—Visa, Mastercard, American Express. None of that Discover Card crap."

Franklin extracted a Visa card from his wallet and passed it through the reader. The machine voice said, "State time, place, and amount of most recent transaction."

Franklin paused a moment, then said, "Around seven PM, J. Paul Saloon, bar tab, about fifteen dollars."

"Invalid entry."

Franklin reddened. "Er, ten PM, Pleasure Island Videos and Novelties, eighty bucks," he said sheepishly.

"Identity confirmed. Entrance permitted." After a brief pause, the machine voice added tartly, "Issue latex gloves to escorting agents."

Fine led the way into the central gallery, through the Hall of Adhesives, Fasteners, and Twine, and up the west escalator to the second floor.

In the middle of a large open space in front of a towering statue of George Washington lay the body of Hemmings Dumont. He was lying on his back with his arms and hands arranged on his chest and the tips of the fingers of his left hand resting in the center of the palm of his right in a T-shape, exactly like a football referee signaling time-out.

The entire area was cordoned off with yellow police tape, and a dozen officers from a Crime Scene Investigation unit were working under bright klieg lights, collecting samples of fibers, hair, stains, DNA, and atmospheric particles with tweezers, brushes, swabs, and small portable vacuums. In one corner, there was a sharp whining sound as a high-speed drill bored into the terrazzo floor.

The head of the forensics team approached Agent Fine. "Sam Hill, Chief of Forensics," he said, and then read from the display screen of a handheld computer. "Here's the preliminary C.S.I. report. Floor samples indicate that this place is a heavily trafficked public space—probably a museum of some sort. There are traces of chewing gum, suntan lotion, and faint rubber scuff marks typical of sneakers and running shoes. That means only one thing: tourists."

Fine and Dandy nodded in assent, but the vivid description seemed to bring the scene to life for Franklin, who had never encountered the sophisticated investigative techniques mastered by modern police forces. Somehow, he could clearly visualize the crowds milling sheep-like through the galleries earlier in the day.

"We have his dental chart filled in," Hill continued. "We've located his dentist in Bethesda, Maryland, and staked out his house. His clothes were all bought at the Macy's in Tysons Corner—the store manager is in custody. Dumont used an aftershave manufactured at a plant in Gainesville, Ohio—a S.W.A.T. team is going in at oh-seven hundred hours."

"Good work," said Fine.

"He had Chinese take-out food at about nine PM, and we're working on the recipe. It looks like some kind of Hunan shrimp dish, but we're having trouble duplicating the hot pepper sauce." He gestured to a corner of the room where a pair of technicians were stir-frying a pile of ingredients in a sizzling wok over a Bunsen burner.

"Cause of death?" Dandy asked.

"Not a clue," said Hill.

"Poison dart, probably tipped with dianastydethylene."

Fine, Dandy, Franklin, and Hill all turned in unison. An attractive African-American woman in her late twenties, dressed in a jumpsuit, stood quietly next to them. She held up a Ziploc bag. In it was a tiny feathered dart."

"It's a chemical with a distinctive peppery smell used

commercially to dye madras cloth, but it's also a powerful paralytic toxin—fairly slow-acting, but invariably fatal."

"Of course!" Hill exclaimed, striking the base of his hand against his forehead with an audible slap. "That explains the unusual two-inch-diameter circular inflamed welt with concentric rings of mottled bruising we observed on the side of his neck. We thought it might be some as yet unknown form of hickey," he added lamely.

She turned to Agent Fine and flipped open an ID case. "Sandra Damsel, Toxicology Officer, Centers for Disease Control. Something triggered the alarm function in one of our toxin detectors."

"Toxin detectors?" said Dandy.

"Ever since the anthrax and ricin scares, we've had multispectral air scanners located in public places throughout the Capital District."

Franklin did a double take.

"Probably the MSG," said the forensic expert apologetically. "Where did you find that dart?"

Agent Damsel gestured across the room. In the middle of the opposite wall, scrawled in large, shaky felt-tip pen strokes, were the words LOOK HERE FIRST. An arrow below them pointed to a low metal guard's stool, which still held Dumont's wallet. "He would have had at least fifteen minutes before total paralysis. He probably pulled it out of his neck, but it wouldn't have done any good—the poison is absorbed instantly."

She gave the bagged dart to Agent Hill. "He also left a note," Damsel said, handing over a piece of ordinary printer paper. On it was a row of four simply drawn images: a coiled garden hose with a little spray of droplets coming out of the nozzle; a hay bale; a canoe; and a line of waves with a couple of stylized seagull shapes flying overhead. Below, on a separate line, was a sketch of a classic skeleton key with an oval circlet at one end and old-fashioned square-cut teeth at the other.

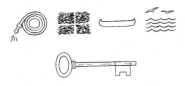

"What the hell is that?" Dandy asked.

"I think it's a rebus," said Sandra Damsel. "A puzzle where each picture stands for a syllable in a word."

Hill scratched his head. "That's a tough nut to crack," he said. "We'll scan it and send it over to the National Security Agency—they can break any code known to man." He lowered his voice to a whisper. "Just last week, they managed to decipher the hidden charges in a Hertz rental car contract," he confided.

While Fine, Dandy, and Hill studied the weird symbols on the page, Damsel whipped a thin metal wand from a pocket and swept it rapidly over Franklin's shoulders and arms. The instrument immediately began emitting a series of short, sharp shrieks.

"Gentlemen," she said sharply, "this man is exhibiting possible signs of smallcox contamination. I must isolate him temporarily."

Fine and Dandy looked unconvinced.

"In extreme cases, it can cause permanent erectile dysfunction. If you don't believe me, ask Bob Dole," she added ominously.

The three G-men backed away quickly.

Damsel took a suddenly ashen-faced Franklin by the arm and marched him out of the room.

"Smallcox?" he stammered weakly. "Is there a cure?"

"Don't worry," she hissed. "The only thing you're suffering from is an acute case of we-really-need-to-make-a-hasty-exitosis. And for an expeditious egress, I always prescribe a healthy dose of bullshit."

CHAPTER 6

THE STRETCH OF Hill Street that held the tomb-like clubhouse of Yale's Skull and Bones secret society rarely saw much foot traffic at any time of day, but at this hour of the morning, the whole area, like the rest of the sprawling gothic campus, was completely deserted.

With one exception. A slim, almost invisible figure, dressed entirely in black, flitted like a shadow along one of the beige stone walls of the forbidding fortress-like headquarters of one of America's most mysterious institutions.

With its massive masonry block construction and narrow, heavily barred windows, the hokey structure oozed invincibility and obstinate power, but Ben Quick Brown Fox of Connecticut's centuries-old Queequogue Indian tribe snorted dismissively at the sight.

For the twenty-two-year-old former Army Ranger, who had once rappelled down a 200-foot cliff in Tora Bora to snatch a Taliban commander from his mountain hideout, burglarizing this fruit-loop frat house would be about as difficult as breaking into a pup tent with a chain saw.

Even though Quick Brown Fox possessed the requisite skills, he would have seemed to be miscast in the role of second-story man. A grandson of the legendary Chief Tall Cotton, who had used a combination of persistence and guile to gain federal recognition for the poverty-stricken remnants of his once proud tribe, Quick Brown Fox now made over $200,000 a year as head of security at the Caymanasset Nation's gigantic Bearwoods casino.

Chump change. The resort itself grossed $500 million a month. And the work wasn't particularly challenging—the place was surprisingly sedate, and about the biggest thing he'd had to deal with all year was a shipment of computerized voting terminals destined for Florida that had been mistakenly configured as slot machines.

He couldn't help but smile. In one of history's greatest ironies, the white man now came of his own accord directly to the Indians to be scalped, albeit by one-armed bandits instead of tomahawk-wielding braves.

With a powerful but effortless-looking motion, Quick Brown Fox threw the three pronged hardened nickel grappling hook over the building's cornice and rapidly ascended the dark gray Dacron rope attached to the eyelet at the end of its shaft.

He dropped softly onto the roof, pulled up and stowed the rope, then selected the spot on the steel fire stair door to set the high-powered pinpoint demolition charge.

With a barely audible *fumpf,* one hundred grams of pyroxylin thermite ignited, propelling the case-hardened penetrator tip into the thick metal panel, instantly vaporizing the lock, bolt, and latch with a jet of 2,800-degree molten tungsten.

Quick Brown Fox pulled the door open and soundlessly descended the narrow thirteen-step stair. The floor plan he had accessed from the Internet was surprisingly accurate, as was the description of the interior as a gloomy, ratty attic crammed with ten generations' worth of adolescent collegiate souvenirs.

He crossed to the door of the Inner Temple and set

a second compact demolition charge, which punched through the ornate but malleable black metal portal like an awl through soft leather.

He flashed his tiny Maglite torch around the dim, wainscot-covered, painting-lined walls. The beam immediately reflected off the long glass case that held the object of his quest.

He attached a suction-cup handgrip to the lid of the vitrine, then, making a practiced stroke with a diamond-tipped glass cutter, he scored a wide oval, tapped the pane sharply, lifted out the incised section, and extracted the skull of Geronimo.

As he reverently placed the ghoulish trophy in his backpack, he remembered how Ed Talking Horse, the Lakota Sioux he'd trained with at Ranger school, had told him the story of the desecration of the grave of the great Apache warrior at Fort Sill, Oklahoma, in May of 1918, by President Bush's grandfather Prescott and five of his fellow pranksters. Quick Brown Fox had sworn then to recover the sacred artifact and return it to its proper resting place so that the spirit of the great Chiricahua chief could finally rest.

Quick Brown Fox noticed an Apache medicine stick lying on the velvet at the bottom of the case. Another precious tribal relic scavenged by these sacrilegious bone-heads. He added it to his spoils, laying in its place a cryptic message written in crayon on a strip of toilet paper.

S370HSSV–0773H

Less than fifteen minutes later, dressed in nondescript street clothes, he was sitting in New Haven's grimy bus station waiting for the first morning departure to Washington, DC. The new law on Native American artifacts was crystal clear. Once the skull was in the possession of any federal employee, and that included a Smithsonian curator, it had to be returned to its tribe, regardless of how it had been obtained.

The precious parcel was wedged between his feet. He was relieved not to have to go through airport security with that awkward piece of carry-on luggage.

He wondered how long it would take those preppy dipshits to realize that in order to absorb the full meaning of his message, they'd have to turn it upside down.

CHAPTER 7

SANDRA DAMSEL guided Franklin through an inner court that held a suite of rooms with reproductions of White House interiors and up the stairs to the Archives Center at the east end of the building's third floor.

She turned down a corridor, stopped in front of a door marked OFFICE OF THE CURATOR, took out a key, and unlocked it.

"Silly me," she said brightly. "I must have forgotten to turn over Hemmings's keys."

Franklin had been in Dumont's cozy book-lined private office before. He remembered the dismantled antique clocks, the partially assembled colonial-era printing press, and the piles of bobbins, spindles, rotors, flywheels, pinions, gears, and motor parts covering every horizontal surface in mute, if messy, testimony to the inveterate tinkerer's inquiring mind.

"Multispectral toxin detectors?" said Franklin. "Look, I had CBR training back in the army, and I know that's technically impossible—there are too many different compounds, with wildly varying properties, active in an almost infinite number of concentrations. . . ."

Damsel shot him an angry look. "Did you just come up with that out of the blue, or did you actually lay some groundwork?"

"It's way back in chapter one," Franklin said defiantly.

"All right, Professor Franklin, it was all a ruse," she conceded. "I really am a C.D.C. Epidemiological Intelligence Officer with a degree in public health from the University of North Carolina. But I'm not on this case officially, and twenty-dollar Cootie Catchers from Toys 'R' Us are not part of our standard-issue emergency kit." She held up the wand. "I needed to get you out of there, and I needed to talk to you."

"You know my name."

"And you're missing part of mine. It's Sandra H. Damsel—H for Hemmings. Dumont was my uncle."

"That means that just like Dumont, you're a descendant of Thomas Jefferson, from his relationship with the slave girl Sally Hemmings."

"My great-great-great-great-great-grandmother."

Franklin nodded. "I didn't get a chance to tell those feds—they kept peppering me with hostile answers—but that's why Dumont was planning to come to my book signing. I'm working on a new blockbuster tentatively titled *The Monticello Code*. I e-mailed him a few days ago to let him know I was going to be in town. I wanted to pick his brains."

"*Monticello Code?*" Sandra snorted. "Great, more pulp history."

"I prefer to think of it as popular scholarship with a mass appeal," said Franklin, sounding a little hurt. "Get this: Both John Adams and Thomas Jefferson died within hours of each other, hundreds of miles apart, on July fourth, 1826, fifty years practically to the hour after the Declaration of Independence was adopted."

"So you thought you spotted a conspiracy?"

"No, I thought I spotted a bestseller." He frowned. "Listen, your family is proof that Jefferson hid one very big secret. My research has led me to the conclusion that it wasn't the only secret he was hiding, and it wasn't the biggest one, either."

"A secret big enough to get my uncle killed?"

Franklin looked thoughtful. "That's really hard to believe. I mean, why would anyone want to kill a harmless curator for something that happened almost two centuries ago?"

"I don't know," Sandra admitted. "But my uncle must have known he was in danger—he left me a coded message on my cell phone asking me to please come right over after work."

"What did it say?"

" 'Leasepay omecay ightray veroay afterfay orkway.' "

"Pig Latin," said Franklin, admiring the old man's ingenuity. "But what about the rebus and the time-out sign?"

"Oh, that's easy," Sandra said confidently. "I'll explain on the way to the gallery."

"Gallery? What gallery?"

"Why, the gallery where the original Star-Spangled Banner hangs, of course," said Sandra. From Dumont's desk she picked up a copy of a local publication listing Washington events.

"I think he would have wanted us to have this," she said, sticking the copy of the *Time Out Washington* guide into her pocket.

CHAPTER 8

DEWEY CHEATHAM '01–"Ducksy" D.199, as he was known to his fellow Bonesmen–dropped his overnight bag on the bed of his small but comfortable room at the Yale Club, whose imposing twenty-two-story clubhouse across the street from Grand Central Terminal in New York City is often mistaken for a hotel by passersby.

This was not where he had expected to spend the night when he sat in his dorm room at the University of Virginia Law School sixteen hours earlier preparing for a class on backdating documents that made up a large part of his course in Creative Management of Large Estates Mistakenly Left to Widows, Orphans, and Non-Profit Institutions. On the other hand, a Knight—well, he was now a Patriarch himself—never knew when an urgent call to duty might come from one of the Senior Patriarchs.

The instructions had been simple, if enigmatic. Go at once to nearby Monticello and meet with—of all people— one of Thomas Jefferson's great-great-great-great-great-grandsons from the "legitimate" side of the family.

It had been a pleasant drive on a warm sunny day from the elegant classical quadrangle of the Charlottesville campus designed by America's most gifted president to his other great masterpiece, the stunning domed Palladian villa to which he had retired after leaving office.

T. J. "Jeff" Jefferson turned out to be a mousy little man with wispy hair, pale watery eyes, and a weak chin, who could easily have been the poster boy for the perils of generations of inbreeding. He had greeted Cheatham dressed in the colonial costume he wore as a docent at his distinguished ancestor's estate.

Jeff, visibly upset, wasted no time conducting Cheatham into the beautifully proportioned study where the most cerebral of the founding fathers had whiled away the hours writing letters, designing gardens, and engaging in the botanical studies that consumed much of his time in his final years.

Jeff showed Cheatham the hidden compartment in one of the cleverly disguised mahogany wall panels that had somehow escaped discovery for two hundred years, explaining how he had accidentally triggered its intricate spring-loaded catch a day earlier when he knocked over, and broke, a replica of the eighteenth-century brass telescope—the original, fortunately, was now in the Smithsonian—that Jefferson had used to observe the process of construction of his beloved university in the valley below.

His hands shaking, he gave Cheatham a slim vellum folder. Looking inside, Dewey saw it held a single-page letter written in the unmistakable handwriting of the man whose penmanship graces the Declaration of Independence.

"It's a copy of a letter to Colonel William P. Clark," Jeff sputtered, barely able to control his emotions. "That's Clark as in 'Lewis and Clark.' It was written about a month before Jefferson died." He pointed to a peculiar apparatus of hinged and articulated wooden levers and metal fittings mounted on a tilted writing desk.

"It's a pantograph," Jeff explained. "You put a second pen in that clip-thing, slide a sheet of paper underneath, and then when you write the original, the pen strokes are automatically reproduced, and you simultaneously make an exact duplicate."

"Why bother with that contraption?" asked Cheatham. "Why not just jot down a copy?"

Jeff looked at him scornfully. "Have you ever tried to write with a quill pen?" he demanded. "And I don't mean scribble—I mean inscribe perfectly formed cursive letters with constant equal pressure in absolutely straight lines, page after page?"

Cheatham shook his head. Hell, he could barely handle the stylus that came with his PalmPilot.

"It's brutal. In the last two decades of his life, Jefferson suffered from crippling writer's cramp. The fact that he went to the trouble to make these copies means that somewhere, there's a big fat packet of originals."

Cheatham didn't know quite what to say. He cradled the folder gently. "It's obviously a precious historical artifact," he said.

"Precious, yes. But also catastrophic," said Jeff. "We are very fortunate to have one of your, er, members on the board of Monticello. When I contacted him, he instantly understood the importance of this discovery. If that letter is genuine, and I believe it is, and if the documents it refers to exist, it will change history, and infinitely for the worse!"

"I see," said Cheatham, although, of course, he didn't. He had cut most of his history classes.

Jeff was almost crying now. "Those interlopers, those usurpers," he moaned. "That DNA trickery they used to make their wretched claim he mated with a slatternly slave girl—and now this!"

A trickle of casually dressed visitors to Monticello began to file into the study, and as Jeff rose to his feet and struggled to regain his composure, Cheatham backed out of the room.

He drove directly to the airport and took the first flight to LaGuardia. The plane was nearly empty, and once they were airborne, he gingerly extracted the letter and read it, then carefully replaced it in its folder and slipped it back into his bag. *If this ever got out, it could be much worse than that close call in the university archives a couple of years back when his older brother, Howard, found—and quickly destroyed—the only copy of a letter to the college from Adolf Hitler politely declining the offer of an honorary degree from the class of 1940.*

He looked out the window. In the far distance, the brightly lit dome of the Capitol dominated the nighttime skyline of Washington. Howard—also Ducksy, since as a

Bones legacy he shared his sibling's nickname—was somewhere in that ornate building right now, serving as an intern to an influential senator.

Cheatham ordered and consumed three Bloody Marys in rapid succession. *I don't care how hush-hush this is supposed to be—I've got to share this secret with Howie.*

He reached for the Airfone in the back of the headrest of the seat in front of him and punched in the number of the office of Senator Richard Kydd.

Dewey Cheatham took the elevator up to the twenty-second floor, turned left down a narrow corridor, and knocked on a door marked PUMP ROOM. Long ago, some undergraduate in a stupor who had somehow mistaken the out-of-the-way location for the club's popular mezzanine bar had scrawled NOT THE TAP ROOM under the sign. A faint sound of water passing through plumbing was just barely audible.

A voice from inside said, "Who sits to the left of Uncle Toby?"

"Little Devil," Cheatham replied.

The door opened and Schooner Deckshod '39—Patriarch "Skipper" D.137—dressed even in the wee hours of the morning in a three-piece suit, took the folder and waved Cheatham into the cubicle.

Badly injured in a freak spinnaker mishap during the catboat finals on the Wannsee in the 1936 Berlin Olympics, Deckshod had spent the war in the O.S.S., then followed up his service with a career in its successor agency, the C.I.A. He'd helped plan the Bay of Pigs and a number of less well-publicized but equally legendary operations, including the Bog of Dogs, the Fen of Bugs, the Loch of Snakes, the Fjord of Rats, and the Glade of Leeches.

The small room was filled not with pipes but with a massive radio transmitter. A thick copper cable ran through the ceiling past a faded engraved portrait of Nathan Hale, the first—but by no means the last—of Yale's multigenerational bumper crop of deeply incompetent spies. The wire led to a twenty-foot-high long-range antenna cleverly concealed inside a twenty-foot-high microwave tower that protruded from the water tank on the clubhouse roof.

A forty-year-old Grundig reel-to-reel recorder on the floor played an endlessly looped tape of gurgling sounds, which Deckshod had recorded years earlier from the club's actual water delivery system on the one and only trip he would ever make to a basement in his life.

Schooner Deckshod took a seat in a swivel chair, threw a large toggle switch, and twisted a series of dials. The room filled with the subtle odor of hot solder as banks of vacuum tubes began to glow.

Deckshod placed the Jefferson document on a metal stand, rotated the alphabet wheels to engage the high-speed inverter on the encryption machine, and began transmitting the first string of encoded letters of the top secret message.

... EGASSEM TERCES POT

Nine hundred miles to the north, in a huge old stone mansion on the rocky Maine coast, a teletype machine clattered to life.

CHAPTER 9

FRANKLIN FOLLOWED Sandra past an exhibit of *Sesame Street* Muppet costumes and, farther on, a dais holding one of the best-known pieces of furniture in the world: Archie Bunker's faded, mustard-colored armchair from *All in the Family*.

They took the west stairs down to the second floor and slipped into the large, high-ceilinged gallery that housed one of America's most revered relics.

The enormous 30- x 34-foot fifteen-star flag nearly covered one entire wall, its painstakingly preserved stains, tears, and tatters testifying to the heroic resistance of Fort McHenry to the British bombardment of 1814, a proud moment in U.S. military history that had inspired the hard-to-remember and equally difficult-to-sing words of the national anthem.

"Remember the rebus?" Sandra asked.

"Let's see," said Franklin. "A lawn sprinkler, a bale, some kind of boat, and water."

Sandra rolled her eyes. "Hose, Hay, Canoe, Sea," she pronounced impatiently. "O, Say, Can You See."

"OK, what about the key?" said Franklin.

"Francis Scott Key," she said, walking over to a framed sheet of handwritten lyrics exhibited in a glass-topped case nearby. She reached behind the display, ran her hand along the panel in back, and extracted a small brown envelope. Written on the outside was:

"4!"

She opened the flap, turned it upside down, and shook out its contents. A curious brass token about the size of a quarter, with a pair of notches cut in the top and bottom, dropped into her palm. Sandra examined it dumbly.

"I know something you don't know," taunted Franklin in a teasing voice. Sandra glared at him.

"It's a token for a ball-dispensing machine at a golf driving range," Franklin explained. He pointed to the odd inscription. "Fore!" he said, mimicking a golf swing.

Sandra produced the issue of *Time Out* and flipped

through the pages until she came to one with a turned-down corner. At the bottom of a column of listings, an entry had been circled with a black felt-tip pen: HACKER HEAVEN, 24-HOUR DRIVING RANGE. The item gave an address in south Arlington.

"Hole in one?" asked Sandra.

"Beginner's luck," said Franklin. "By the way, there's something I hope you *do* know," he added.

"What's that?"

"I hope you know how we're going to get out of here."

Sandra thought for a moment. "I'm going to help you fly the coop," she said finally.

The Big Bird costume was stuffy and surprisingly heavy. There was a small slit below the beak that gave Franklin some visibility but practically no peripheral vision. Sandra guided him into the elevator, and when the doors opened on the ground floor, she kept a tight grip on one of his large yellow hands.

Fine and Dandy were nowhere in sight, but several other Homeland Security officers were manning the door. The closest one immediately put his hand on his holster.

"OK, lady, you and the chicken, hold it right there," he commanded.

Sandra flashed her C.D.C. identification badge. "We have a possible case of highly infectious Asian bird flu— I can't rule out terrorism," she said urgently. Franklin coughed as loudly as he could inside the bulky feathered outfit.

The officer reeled back in horror. "Yes, biological warfare!" Sandra intoned dramatically, pushing Franklin toward the door. "And the target, an innocent puppet beloved by children everywhere!

"These fiends will stop at nothing," she added grimly.

The agents stepped aside, several of them quickly donning protective masks.

She guided Franklin down the sloping pathway and out onto the sidewalk. Just behind the government sedan that had brought Franklin to the museum sat a two-tone Mini Cooper with a fading DEAN FOR AMERICA sticker on the bumper.

Franklin gave a strangled cry.

"It's a very practical city car," said Sandra petulantly. She opened the back door and pushed Franklin in headfirst, slammed it shut, got behind the wheel, and pulled away from the curb.

"Isn't it Oscar who's supposed to be the grouchy one?" she asked as his curses filled the tiny vehicle.

CHAPTER 10

THE REMARKABLY fit-looking octogenarian dressed in a terrycloth bathrobe with *41* embroidered on its pocket paced restlessly through the imposing but surprisingly homey living room of the massive seaside mansion.

Through the floor-to-ceiling windows, the softly rolling ocean sparkled in the pale yellow glow of a waning moon. *A thousand points of light. Darn fine phrase, whatever the heck it meant.*

Until that blankety-blank, pardon-my-French teletype had come in, he'd been in a terrific mood. He'd spent a great day, had a grand time. Played eighteen holes of golf in two hours flat, took the speedboat out for a forty-five-mile-per-hour spin on the old briny, did the fishing thing—

never saw the point in it, though. Took so much time to get Mr. Bass to hook up and get with the program.

Back to the hacienda for a few cutthroat games of horseshoes with the summer set—fun folks!—then sundowners on the patio, din-din with the missus down in K-port at the Lobster Trap—top-notch chow!—then back to the shack to watch a movie on that BVD thingy—what was the name of that horse flick—*Sea Muffin? Sea Monkey?*—great yarn! Then to top it all off, old Windpipes comes on the horn from Wash-town with great news! Boola-boola! Score one for the good guys!

Hit the hay humming the Fight Song, sweet dreams—top of the ninth, Yale leads by one, two out, two on, Poppy gets set to pitch, and—*breeeep!*

The Urgent Communication Signal. Sayonara shuteye. Take the old ankle express down to the little communication closet under the stairs. The ancient teletype printer chattering away. Gosh, the secrets that old ticker had spat out over the years! The warning to his grandfather in April of '29 to get out of the market pronto, the heads-up from Tokyo on Thanksgiving in '41, the thoughtful little tip to not bother going all the way down to New Haven on November 22, 1963, for the Harvard-Yale game . . .

He reread the piece of paper, still curled and slightly damp from the teletype printer, then balled it up and threw it onto the pile of still flickering embers in the yawning field-stone fireplace. It smoldered briefly, then burst into flames.

Doggone it! It was like dealing with those dratted moles. Bop one on the head, another pops right up. What was the deal with Thomas Frigging Jefferson, anyway? Darn fellow had a screw loose. Not a sound man, not a team player at all. Took that "all men are created equal" stuff much too seriously.

Got to call Dick Cheney in the A.M. The Boy was in deep doo-doo.

The plump, matronly white-haired lady in a simple cashmere caftan stood at a long counter in the mansion's spacious scullery. Built in an era when all the family meals were prepared and served by a sizable staff of cooks and butlers, it was far larger than even the most grandiose kitchen in a pretentious modern McMansion.

It had hundreds of square feet of counter space, walls of glass-fronted cabinets that now held dozens of stuffed owls and ravens, a walk-in freezer with zinc fittings, a message board that had once recorded summonses for maids from the twenty-odd bedrooms upstairs, a five-thousand-bottle wine cellar with a false pantry shelf-front dating from Prohibition, and, in one corner, a lovely old coal-fired potbelly stove that now held a mammoth iron cauldron bubbling with a pungent-smelling brew from which the bone of a large animal protruded.

The Salem witch from whom the mistress of the house was directly descended would have had to painstakingly chop the various herbs, worts, toadstools, bat wings, and dried snakeskins by hand, but her twenty-first-century progeny used a heavy-duty electric food processor.

As the circular blade whirred, she punched the button on a boom box, and a CD of the ancient Wiccan chants performed by her favorite group of sorcerers, the Coven Spoonful, began to wail eerily. *Thank badness for these labor-saving devices.*

As the potion began to emulsify and emit faint green vapors, she crossed the room and gave the pot a few quick stirs. It was Lynne Cheney's recipe. The concoction certainly had worked its magic in the Florida elections, but who knew whether it would have any effect on those stupid opinion polls.

She put down the ladle, strode over to a large candle-lit altar placed on top of an old enamel hand-mangle washing tub, and stuck another long silver needle into the amazingly lifelike wax-museum-quality doll of Hillary Rodham Clinton.

Take that, Miss Smarty Pants.

CHAPTER 11

AS THE MINI COOPER sped along the Mall, Franklin struggled to extricate himself from the Muppet outfit.

"Are you sure that running away from a bunch of federal agents was a smart thing to do?" he asked, tugging a leg out of the tight-fitting getup.

"It beats spending the next couple of years in solitary confinement in an army brig," Sandra said. She pointed out the window to a large highway sign on the approach ramp to the 14th Street Bridge:

EXIT (CLASSIFIED)

FT. LESLEY MCNAIR

"That's where they were going to take you—it's headquarters for the Washington Military District."

"What!" Franklin exclaimed, spitting out a tiny yellow feather. "Wait, I'm not guilty of anything!"

"Patriot Act, Unreported Paragraph Four, Section Someone Neglected to Mention Six: 'Indefinite detention of a material witness to an overt act alleged to have been committed or contemplated, under presumption of accusation or supposition of insinuation, or on the grounds that we just feel like it.' "

"You're joking," Franklin sputtered.

"Certainly not," Sandra replied in mock outrage. "It's a felony to make jocular and/or derisive remarks about any statute related to national security."

"Holy shit!" Franklin croaked.

"Expressions of shock and awe, even if mildly scatological, are permitted," she added sarcastically.

The brightly lit driving range sat at the far end of a parking lot across the street from a razor wire–lined self-storage company in a desolate stretch of warehouses, auto body shops, and plumbing and electrical supply houses. Tall nets intended to trap errant golf shots surrounded three sides of the aging wooden structure.

Sandra parked the little car by the front door. The place looked deserted, but the door was open, and from inside came the regular *thwock* of golf balls being struck off a rubber mat.

In the only one of the hitting stalls that was occupied, a middle-aged black man was methodically drilling drives out to the end of the weed-covered range. Just short of the 300-yard marker, there was a tight cluster of range balls.

He rested the club on a stand. "Help you?" he said.

Sandra handed him the brass token. He examined it carefully.

"Friends of Mr. Dumont?" he asked.

"He was my uncle," said Sandra.

"Was?"

"He's dead—murdered."

The man shook his head sadly. "You Sandra?" he asked.

Sandra nodded. "Vernon Mount," he said, politely touching his hand to the brim of his battered golf hat. It held the logo of the prestigious Washington National Country Club. He noticed Franklin staring at the famous Capitol dome emblem.

"Caddy there now and then," said Mount.

He ushered Sandra and Franklin into a small office. High on one wall, an ultraviolet bug zapper glowed eerily, and every now and then a moth fizzled wetly against the electric killing screen. Standing beneath it was an old battered ball-dispensing machine with an OUT OF ORDER sign hanging on its front.

Mount put a wire bucket in the hopper, inserted the token into a metal slide, and pushed it in. After a short pause, a grapefruit-size dark plastic globe dropped into the metal basket with a thud. Mount reached over, retrieved the shiny black sphere, and handed it to Sandra. It was a Magic 8 Ball.

"Most likely answer all your questions," said Mount.

CHAPTER 12

THE CREDITS ROLLED at the end of the late-night rerun of *Judge Judy,* and Justice Antonin Scalia turned off the television. *That gal has her head screwed on right, unlike that ditsy Ginsburg dame.*

As usual, he was burning the midnight oil. He'd never needed much sleep, a trait that had stood him in good stead over the years, helping him to secure a coveted position on the law review at Harvard Law School, to become the youngest attorney ever to make partner at one of the nation's top legal firms, and finally to be named to the Supreme Court, where he had quickly gained recognition as one of the most influential conservative voices in the history of American jurisprudence.

He settled back in the stiff-framed mahogany-and-leather chair. It had been a thoughtful, if somewhat tongue-in-cheek, gift from President Reagan, who had rescued the historic electric chair from San Quentin when California abolished the death penalty.

Scalia always did his best thinking in the old "hot seat," and now, as he read through his well-thumbed and heavily annotated copy of the Constitution, he remembered the trip he had taken earlier that year with the vice president.

Hunting whooping cranes with bazookas sounds unsporting, but only to some bleeding-heart gun-hating Audubon Society wimp. For one thing, the warheads aren't heat-seeking, and they were using low-power quarter-kilo training loads set to detonate only on impact—no proximity fuses and no shrapnel casings.

True, you could usually hear the ponderous water-birds coming from a mile away—their telltale shrill calls were as loud as a car alarm—and even if they were flying very high or the wind was wrong, the urgent twitter of the portable radar set gave enough warning to allow you time to shoulder the launcher and take a bead.

But, hey, this wasn't like shooting fish in a barrel. (He knew, because he and Cheney had done just that the previous summer in Crawford—a real hoot, and tougher than it sounds, particularly if you're gunning for trout fingerlings with a .45.) His first rocket had passed way under the flock and landed in an arroyo about a mile away, where it turned a towering saguaro cactus into guacamole.

Cheney had hit one of the trailing birds at the tail end of the wide V-formation right in the center of one wing, but the round was a dud, and the damn thing had barely flinched.

Time for only one last shot. Scalia aligned the tip of the aiming tube with an imaginary point just ahead of the lead bird, pressed the firing button, and held his breath as the missile streaked toward its target. It detonated with a soft *crump,* and the mighty crane exploded in a cloud of white plumage like a split-open sackful of down stuffing in a pillow fight.

"Bull's-eye!" Cheney had said admiringly. "Now if you can just do that to the Constitution."

CHAPTER 13

SANDRA WEIGHED the popular children's toy in her hand. It had a very familiar feel. Her uncle Hemmings had given her one of the silly "fortune-telling" globes for her eighth birthday. You thought of a question, then you shook the ball, turned it over, and looked in the little glass window on its bottom. There, floating in blue liquid, a tiny printed card would bob into view with a mock serious response, like "Answer hazy—ask again later" or "My sources say 'No.'"

She gave the ball a shake, then turned it over and read the first message.

Franklin peered over her shoulder. "What does it say?" he asked.

Sandra squinted at the fine-print type. She recited the enigmatic inscription:

SO MANY TWISTS TO SPIN OUR TALE

"Huh?" said Franklin. "What the heck does that mean?"

Repeating the procedure, Sandra inverted the orb and read out the next pronouncement:

OUR STORY NEEDS TO COME FULL CIRCLE

Franklin snorted. "That really helped."

Sandra tried again:

A YARN LIKE THIS MUST HAVE SOME THREADS

And again:

YOU HAVE REACHED A TURNING POINT

Again:

LOOK AROUND FOR SOME CONNECTION

Again:

THE KNOWLEDGE LIES WITHIN YOUR SPHERE

Again:

YOU MIGHT TRY DOING THINGS BY HALVES

Franklin groaned. "This is getting us nowhere," he groused.

"Let's try one more," said Sandra, not sounding very hopeful. She gave the ball a particularly violent shake, then read the new communication:

OH PLEASE UNSCREW THIS STUPID THING

Sandra held the 8 Ball a few inches from her face and examined it carefully. Around its midsection was a thin, practically invisible seam. Grasping the ball tightly in both hands, she twisted the top away from the bottom with a firm counterclockwise motion. After one complete turn, the two hemispheres separated smoothly.

"Magic," said Mount.

Franklin whistled softly. Neatly nestled in the hollow core of the upper half of the ball sat a mini compact disc. Sandra removed it. Underneath was another of Dumont's ticket-size manila envelopes. She opened it and removed a plastic access card for the self-storage warehouse across the street and a Master padlock key. On the outside of the envelope, in the by-now-familiar felt-tip pen, Dumont had written:

BY TWOS WITH THIS ENUMERATION
WE DO EXPRESS APPRECIATION

Franklin groaned. "Here we go again."

"It must be a clue to the P.I.N. code that opens the outer gate," she said. "They're always four-digit numbers." Sandra turned the envelope over. It was blank on the other side. She peered inside. Blank.

"We need to know the number of his storage bay, too," said Sandra. "That place must have a hundred of them, and half of them probably have Master padlocks. It could take hours to find the right one, and anyone passing by who sees us trying our key in every single one of them is definitely going to call the cops."

Sandra looked closely at the key. The round end was

coated on one side with what looked like nail polish. "This could be invisible ink," she said. "I've got a blacklight reader in the car." She started toward the door.

"I'll get it," said Franklin. "Opening a car door is one puzzle I think I'm capable of solving."

Sandra handed him the car keys. "You'll have to figure out how to open the glove compartment, too," she said dryly.

His head still spinning, Franklin went out to the Mini Cooper, unlocked the passenger-side door, reached in, and popped open the glove compartment.

As he began to rummage through the ridiculously small storage space, he felt the tip of a knife blade against the back of his neck.

"Give me the keys—now!" said a sharp voice with a light but unmistakable Spanish accent.

Still crouching, Franklin passed back the car keys. "Turn around, real slow," said the voice.

Franklin did as he was told. Two slender men, both wearing ski masks and each with an evil-looking stiletto in his right hand, stood on either side of him.

"Wallet," the second mugger ordered, making an impatient "gimme" gesture with his left hand.

Franklin didn't hesitate. He pulled out his battered leather billfold and handed it over.

"Hey, man, look at the ring on his finger," said the first mugger. He reached over and grabbed Franklin's hand roughly, pulling it up to his face for a closer view of the piece of gold jewelry with its curious insignia.

He suddenly rocked backward, as if he'd been punched.

"¡Madre de dios!" he cried. *"¡El signo del diablo! ¡Vámanos!"*

The two carjackers jumped into the Mini, started it up, and sped out of the parking lot.

Franklin was in a state of shock. The whole heist had taken all of two minutes.

Shuffling like a zombie, Franklin stumbled back into Mount's office.

"I've got some bad news and some good news," squeaked Franklin. "The bad news is, a pair of thugs just stole my wallet. The good news is I'm not going to have to ride one more block in your miniature torturemobile."

Sandra gave him an inquiring look. "They took the car, too," said Franklin gloomily.

She came over and put a hand on his shoulder. "You all right?"

"Nothing that ordinary beverage alcohol, taken internally, can't eventually cure, Nurse Damsel," he said, smiling.

She gave his shoulder a reassuring pat. "Doesn't matter—we had to ditch the car anyway. It's too easy to spot. And if we're lucky, your stickup men will use your credit card sometime very soon in some place not too close."

"Twenty-four-hour Mall-Mart about two miles from here," said Mount.

Franklin didn't follow this particular piece of logic and promptly gave up trying.

"I didn't get the UV light," he said, suddenly remembering why he had gone to the car in the first place. "Now we can't read the key."

"Ultraviolet?" Mount asked. He held out a huge hand. Puzzled, Sandra gave him the padlock key they'd found in the Magic 8 Ball. Mount took a small stepladder, set it up under the bug zapper, climbed up two steps, and held the key up to the purplish light.

" 'Ex-ivy sum,' " he read, pronouncing the words carefully. He climbed down and handed back the key.

"Mr. Mount, you're a genius!" Sandra exclaimed.

Franklin rubbed his forehead. "Ivy? Ivy League, maybe. Where did your uncle go to college?"

"Brown," said Sandra. "He used to make the same joke

at every college reunion—'I'm a Brown man and I'm a brown man.' Drove those turkeys crazy."

" 'Sum'—I suppose that means number," said Franklin. He blinked his eyes and tried to clear his head. "Sorry, my Latino friends really messed with my brain—"

He stopped in midsentence. "Latin—it's Latin!"

He took a pencil and a piece of scrap paper from Mount's desk and wrote:

XIV

" 'Ex Eye Vee.' It's the Roman numeral for fourteen. *Sum* is from the Latin verb 'to be.' It means 'I am.' "

Sandra clapped her hands in delight. "Bill Franklin, you're a genius, too!" she said.

"Well, I'm glad someone appreciates me, after all I've been through—"

Once again he stopped short.

"Who do we appreciate?" he said excitedly.

Sandra gave him a blank look.

"Two-four-six-eight," said Franklin triumphantly. He mimed the motion of licking a finger and inscribing an imaginary tick mark on a scorecard. "Score another one for the Nutty Professor."

Sandra gave him a kiss.

———

"Quick, someone, give me another puzzle," said Franklin, laughing.

Mount stood up. "Take you over to the storage yard," he said.

He ushered them outside, turned off the lights, put up a CLOSED sign, and locked the front door. When he came out, Franklin noticed he was carrying a 5-iron. Mount gave it a twirl. "Never know, might have to give some lessons in etiquette."

They walked across the empty parking lot to Mount's car. It was an immense, beautifully maintained 1984 Cadillac. "I like a big car," said Mount.

"I know what you mean," said Franklin.

CHAPTER 14

GASPAR AND MELCHOR Reyes drove Sandra Damsel's Mini Cooper into the vast parking lot of the Mall-Mart supercenter on the Leesburg Pike in Baileys Crossroads. They parked near an exit at the far end of the lot, which even at this hour of the night was nearly a quarter filled with the cars of shopaholic insomniacs browsing for duffel bag–size packages of potato chips, sixty-pound jars of pickles, and industrial drums of mixed nuts.

One of the cashiers on the night shift was their half-brother, Baltasar, who, for a generous cash consideration, would neglect to examine his two relatives' IDs too closely as they came through his checkout line with a shopping cart full of expensive, portable, easy-to-resell electronic goods.

Yes, it was a little risky, but the money was good, and, *Dios,* Melchor and Gaspar were family. They'd escaped from Cuba together in 2000 in the same leaky fishing boat. And if someone asked questions, well, Baltasar could handle it. He was a little loco. Maybe a lot loco. After all, he had been the only one who had laughed out loud when they threw that whining Elián Gonzalez *maricón* overboard in an inner tube.

Gaspar and Melchor checked to make sure Baltasar was on duty—there he was, at #18, right in the middle of the block-long bank of cash registers—then went straight to the back of the gigantic store. They needed only five minutes to assemble $5,000 worth of digital cameras, PalmPilots, cell phones, portable computers, and disk players, but they spent another few moments at the front of the store, idly surveying the gunny sacks of candy, killing time until Baltasar's lane was clear of customers.

The instant it opened up, Gaspar expertly maneuvered the goody-laden cart into place and unloaded the purchases. Baltasar, poker-faced, rang up the loot, and as Melchor swiped Professor Franklin's Visa card through the card reader, he mimed a close inspection of Franklin's picture on his California driver's license, which bore as much resemblance to either of his siblings as Charlie Rose did to Ricky Ricardo.

Within 1.2 seconds, a computer in Rapid City, South Dakota, had registered the transaction. It took another 2.5 seconds to notify the National Financial Systems Surveillance Center in Easton, Maryland, that the credit card trace had located the Priority Alpha Search Subject at a Mall-Mart in Virginia, just outside the Arlington city limits.

Three minutes later, the Marine Chinook helicopter assigned to the Department of Homeland Security for Emergency Standby Duty lifted off from Fort McNair with a Joint Interdepartmental Crisis Team. It covered the ten miles to Baileys Crossroads in six minutes.

The lumbering twin-rotored craft landed in the center of an empty handicapped parking area near the front entrance of the megastore. Agents Fine and Dandy, who had been heading the hunt for Professor Franklin from the Potomac-side army base, were the first down the ramp, followed by a heavily armed Special Forces S.W.A.T. team.

As they moved toward the store, a separate unit of crack combat public relations officers disembarked from the copter and deployed across an unoccupied section of the parking lot, where they cordoned off a large area with velvet ropes, set up a podium, a bank of television lights, a dozen American flags, a blue backdrop cloth imprinted with the logo of the Homeland Security Agency and emblazoned with the catchphrase "Making America Nervous," and three rows of metal folding chairs for the press conference where the capture of one of the nation's most wanted fugitives would shortly be announced.

And in vivid illustration of the ongoing jurisdictional disputes that still plagued the fledgling superagency entrusted with the nation's domestic security, an officer of the Department of Transportation booted one of the helicopter's huge wheels for parking in a restricted zone, an F.A.A. supervisor ticketed the pilot for a nonfunctioning navigational light, and a sharp-eyed Coast Guard lieutenant suspended himself, with pay, when he discovered that the floatability certification of his life vest had expired.

Gaspar and Melchor were still standing by the register, and they were starting to get restless. It rarely took this long for the approval code to come through, even for an out-of-state card. Suddenly, Baltasar's eyes widened in shock as six infantrymen in full combat gear surrounded the three brothers, pointing their loaded M-16s directly at the heads of the trio of stunned felons.

As astonished shoppers backed away from the scene, a

soothing voice came on the public address system. "Ladies and gentlemen, agents from the Department of Homeland Security are conducting a routine seizure of one of the world's most dangerous individuals. There is no cause for anything other than mild trepidation bordering on moderate disquiet, blended with a certain amount of justifiable anxiety, mingled with an overall sense of considerable, but not excessive, alarm. Please continue shopping normally! Remember, if we don't take advantage of the incredible bargains being offered in this fine retail outlet, the terrorists will have won!"

Reassured, a handful of patrons peeled off to stock up on jumbo rolls of duct tape the diameter of truck tires, forklift pallet–loads of Dinty Moore Beef Stew, and crates of fear-scented candles.

Agent Dandy held out a blowup of a file photograph of Franklin from the Passport Agency. "The fugitive academic pictured here almost certainly had his wallet stolen sometime in the last hour at this location in the Washington metro area," he barked.

"Just a minute, Jim," Agent Fine interrupted. "We haven't read them the Miranda warning. The *Carmen* Miranda warning," he added sternly.

Dandy cleared his throat. "Yes, you have no civil rights—you have no civil rights today, no way!"

Fine took up the recitation. "Yes, you can't call a lawyer—you can't call a lawyer today, no way!"

"Yes, you can't remain silent—you can't remain silent today, no way!" Dandy continued.

"Yes, you'll never leave Guantánamo, you'll never leave Guanánamo Bay, no way!" Fine concluded.

Baltasar erupted in fury. "Cuba! They will send us back to Cuba! *¡Idiota! ¡Estúpido!*" He gripped Melchor firmly around the throat with both hands and began to strangle his panic-stricken kinsman. "Tell them or I will kill you!"

Dandy turned to Fine. "I know they're supposed to provide us with all the questions, but is it OK for them to conduct the interrogation, too?"

Fine watched as Melchor's eyes bulged in their sockets and his face started to turn blue. "No problem, as long as he stays within operational guidelines on the use of physical force," he stated in a tone of authority.

"The 1949 Geneva Convention?" asked Dandy.

"Negative, Jim," said Fine menacingly. "The 1968 Chicago Convention."

CHAPTER 15

MOUNT ROLLED DOWN his window, inserted the plastic access card into the slot on the unmanned kiosk at the entrance to the self-storage lot, and punched 2-4-6-8 on the keypad. The gate immediately swung open.

Franklin, who had been perched at the edge of his seat during the process, sat back heavily with a sigh of relief.

"So much for the math quiz," he said. "Now let's hope I do as well on the Latin exam."

Mount parked outside a storage bay marked with a large numeral 14. Sandra got out and tried the key in the massive bronze padlock that secured the steel garage-style roll-down door to the heavy iron frame. The lock popped open with a satisfying *snak*.

Mount and Franklin heaved on the corrugated metal shutter and rattled it partway open. Ducking under the half-raised door, the three entered the stuffy cubicle.

Franklin felt along the wall for a light switch, found it, and flipped it on, lighting the single bare bulb mounted in the center of the ceiling of the compartment.

The chamber looked like some demented modern version of the discovery of King Tut's tomb. It was jam-packed with every imaginable kind of American folk art collectible: a horse-and-carriage weather vane, a pair of long wooden telemark skis with leather strap bindings, a butter churn, a two-handed ice saw for cutting up a frozen pond into blocks, a shelf of apothecary jars, a cider press, a wire rack filled with nickel Coke bottles, a crate of wooden duck decoys, a harpoon, an antique railroad depot sign, a box of green glass telegraph insulators, a hand-cranked coffee bean grinder, and a soapstone washtub.

The stale air smelled vaguely of mildew.

"Man was a pack rat," said Mount affectionately. "Couldn't pass a yard sale. Even has the kitchen sink."

Sandra groaned. "Somewhere in this unholy mess, there's a computer this disc from the Magic 8 Ball will run on," she said. She held up the CD, and as the light from the single bulb reflected off it, something caught her eye.

"Wait a minute," she said. "There's some tiny letters scratched into the nonplaying side."

Franklin stepped over for a closer look. Squinting, he spelled out the inscription:

A

P

P

L

J U I C E

Sandra rolled her eyes in dismay. "I am *so* not in the mood for a treasure hunt," she groused.

"Think I see the juice," said Mount. He pointed to a brown extension cord that snaked its way from the storage room's sole receptacle under the light switch to the bottom of the antique cider press. The wire was barely visible against the dark wooden slats of the old-fashioned screw-operated apple crusher as it ran up and into the spout at the base of its barrel-shaped pulp receptacle.

Franklin lifted the lid of the juice extractor and pulled out a Macintosh iBook laptop computer. He set it on top of a dilapidated rolltop desk standing nearby and flipped up the screen. "And this would be the Apple," he said.

He hit the power button, waited for the desktop display to fill in, then selected the icon for the compact disc drive. The CD holder slid open, and he pressed the disc from the Magic 8 Ball into place in the circular recess in the compartment and pushed it shut.

With an audible whirring sound, the CD loaded its contents into the laptop's RAM memory. The screen displayed a simple dialog box.

" 'Enter Password,' " said Franklin, reading from the screen. "Five letters. Too bad," he added sourly. "I had a whole lot of four-letter words I'd really like to have tried."

Sandra stood very still for a long moment, lost in thought. She could almost smell the deadly spiked hot toddy her uncle used to brew each autumn.

"Try C-I-D-E-R," she suggested.

Franklin typed it in.

The screen went blank for a moment, then filled with a close-up image of the familiar figure of Hemmings Dumont, nattily dressed in a blue blazer and a yellow bow tie, seated at his Smithsonian office desk.

"Hello," said the dead man.

CHAPTER 16

IT WAS TWO in the morning on one of the rare nights in the past few months that the Democratic presidential candidate was able to spend in his own bed in his historic town house on Boston's fashionable Beacon Hill, and John Kerry was wide awake.

It had been a grueling week on the campaign trail, and he was utterly exhausted, but for some unknown reason he simply could not make himself fall asleep.

He'd tried counting primary sweeps. He'd counted the number of times he'd mentioned his Vietnam War combat record in his most recent press conference. He'd counted all the different positions he'd taken on both sides of every major issue. It was no use.

He got up and went downstairs to the elegant residence's immaculate Poggenpohl-designed kitchen. Maybe a glass of soy milk and some low-carb cookies would do the trick. And he could always play a tape of one of his stump speeches. They made everyone else nod off—it might have the same effect on him.

He carried the milk and a plate of cookies into his office, set them down on an end table, and turned on the light. Curled up in the middle of his desk was a large black cat. Kerry did not own a cat. His temperamental wife, Teresa, hated the things.

The cat opened its eyes. "Message for Senator John Kerry," it said in a clear voice.

Kerry froze. He pinched himself, hard. It hurt. He took a bite of cookie. It crunched. *I'm not dreaming.*

"How can you eat those things? They taste like puppy biscuits," said the cat, wrinkling its nose in disgust. "And *soy* milk? Why not just drink a can of white paint?"

"Who—what are you?" Kerry stammered. "And how did you get into my house?"

The cat sat up. "I am a catsimile," it said. "Most firms use faxes for important communications, but my organi-

zation prefers to send cats. A cat gets the recipient's attention. And cats *do* like a lot of attention," it added briskly.

"And exactly what might that organization be?" demanded Kerry, regaining his composure and reverting to
his customary snotty attitude.

"We're the Brimstone Group," the cat declared, as if
reciting the text of a corporate identity ad. "We make very
long-term investments in human resources. Our goal is to
build enduring, mutually beneficial relationships with individuals looking for an ironclad guarantee of success and
prosperity in an uncertain world. If you're among those
exceptional people who are willing to give their all to get
ahead, we have a hell of a deal for you."

In an instinctive response dating back to his days in
Catholic school, Kerry started to make the sign of the
cross but caught himself and pretended to scratch his forehead.

"We also run a crabgrassroots issue-advocacy committee called Giveadamn.org that works to elect candidates
who agree to support key elements of our program," the
cat continued.

"And pray tell, what is your program?" Kerry asked
snidely. "Medicare for pets? Cat food stamps? Kitty litter
laws?"

The cat ignored the gibe. "No 'sin taxes,' strong opposition to any legislation permitting challenges to binding personal service contracts, a ban on drilling extremely deep geothermal wells, and a presidential pardon for Martha Stewart," it said, underscoring each item of the agenda by tapping one paw on the toes of the other.

"I want to make it absolutely clear that in an America with a heart, forgiveness is as much a part of justice as vengeance," Kerry intoned, ad-libbing a policy statement on the spot. "There is a difference between a simple mistake and a serious crime, and if an excessive penalty is imposed by a vindictive judge on a hardworking woman who single-handedly enriched the lifestyle of an entire nation—"

"OK, OK, enough!" cried the cat, covering its ears with its paws. "You're eligible for a possible endorsement."

"And precisely what benefit would such an endorsement confer?" Kerry asked haughtily.

"Let's put it this way," said the cat slyly. "In a close election you would be amazed at how much havoc a team of highly trained gremlins can wreak in a room full of touch-screen voting machines."

The cat stood up on all fours, stretched, yawned, and walked to the edge of Kerry's desk. "Feline Communications Commission regulations require me to state that if

you were sent this cat in error or if you do not wish to receive any further cats from us in the future, you may call
our twenty-four-hour toll-free number, 866-666-1313, to
have your name deleted from our tabbyfax database."

The cat jumped lightly to the floor and vanished.
Kerry pinched himself again. It still hurt. He went to a
window and looked out at the floodlit golden dome of the
Massachusetts State House.

*"An America with a heart." I really should work that phrase into
my inaugural address.*

CHAPTER 17

"I AM HEMMINGS DUMONT," said the face on the small screen of the laptop computer. Dumont spoke without notes, but on the desk in front of him was a pile of eighteenth-century parchment documents, their curling ends held flat by paperweights.

"I am a direct descendant of Sally Hemmings, the slave girl at Monticello with whom Thomas Jefferson had an intimate relationship, which resulted in the birth of several children of mixed race.

"Sometime towards the end of June 1826, a week or two before his death on July fourth of that year, Jefferson summoned Sally Hemmings into his study and entrusted to her care a collection of extraordinary documents.

"Whether he was animated by a spirit of remorse, or was simply acting out of a desire to tidy up his tangled affairs and perhaps set himself right with his Creator, we simply have no way of knowing.

"Whatever his motivation," Dumont continued, "he bequeathed to Sally and her descendants a unique—and potentially quite explosive—legacy. No doubt she and the other slaves on Jefferson's estate would have preferred to be given their freedom, a generous gesture which members of the Virginia aristocracy, like George Washington himself, usually provided for in their wills. Probably due to the precarious state of his finances, this Thomas Jefferson failed to do."

Dumont gestured reverently at the stack of parchments. "Even today, the contents of this legacy are truly flabbergasting, and it is hard not to speculate at the astonishment they must have caused the literate but far from educated slave girl.

"The first of the manuscripts is a confidential letter written by President George Washington on the last day of his second term, addressed to all his successors, informing them that the critical financial and, ultimately, military support for the foundering colonial cause in the terrible

Valley Forge winter of 1777–1778 came from France, via the Marquis de Lafayette, as the result of what was, in effect, a pact with the devil. The terms of the covenant obliged the future occupants of the nation's highest office to provide to 'the Supreme Potentate of the Nether Regions, or such of his Nominees or Viceroys as he may see fit to Appoint' direct, timely, and unfettered access to the President, in perpetuity.

"The second portion of the legacy consists of a sheaf of love letters that clearly show that at least three, and possibly five, of the founding fathers, certainly including Jefferson himself, Madison, and Monroe, and probably John Adams, had engaged in a variety of homosexual relationships during the heady early days of the Revolution.

"The third, and by far the most significant, part of the gift is an amended deed for the Louisiana Purchase, executed by Jefferson while still president, and witnessed and approved by Chief Justice Marshall of the Supreme Court, in which Jefferson used his plenipotentiary power to amend the terms, transforming the transaction into a two-hundred-year lease, upon whose expiration in October of 2003, the entire 828,000 square miles would devolve to any and all descendants of African slaves then living in the United States."

Dumont paused for effect. "I have examined these

documents exhaustively, and I can vouch absolutely for their authenticity.

"For nearly two centuries, over seven generations, through war, persecution, and economic upheaval, the Hemmings family has carefully preserved this peculiar inheritance, revealing its existence only when a new custodian—or Keeper—is selected.

"The secret remained safe until sometime last year. An aide conducting research in the Library of Congress for Senator Richard Kydd—who is an accomplished amateur historian as well as the dean of the Democratic Party in the Senate—apparently stumbled on a miscataloged handwritten journal kept by Jefferson. It must have been included, probably by mistake, in the collection of 6,500 books that the perpetually cash-strapped Jefferson sold to the library in 1814 for $24,000. In that journal, there was a cryptic reference to Washington's letter and to the Louisiana deed.

"Senator Kydd called me directly and asked for the assistance of the Smithsonian archives in researching this fascinating historical footnote. The senator is a notorious master of the appropriations process—he didn't get the nickname 'Captain Kydd, the Pirate of Pork' for nothing— but he is a man of complete integrity, a stalwart champion of the rights and prerogatives of the Senate, a fierce defender of the Constitution, and an implacable foe of unchecked presidential power. I am torn on how to proceed, since, of course, I am the current Keeper.

"Over the last few weeks, I have been followed and my office and home have been broken into several times—always very professionally, with nothing stolen. I am quite certain my phone is tapped. Obviously, there are powerful interests that would quite literally stop at nothing to prevent these documents from ever seeing the light of day.

"I'm equally certain that Senator Kydd has nothing to do with any of this. He probably has a spy in his office, which is hardly surprising considering his vocal opposition to the current administration.

"The documents are hidden safely, though in plain sight.

"Here is a clue that will help guide you to their whereabouts:

There once was a dandy called doodle
With a cap plume named after a noodle;
That pasta's my address;
His nag's breed will access
The fast mail that leads to the boodle.

"I wish I could advise you how to proceed, but I simply do not know.

"I say 'you' because if you're listening to this little lecture, I am almost certainly already dead.

"Have a nice day!"

Sandra, Franklin, and Mount sat speechless as the screen went blank and was replaced by the happy–Mac Apple operating system icon.

"Man said a mouthful," said Mount. He stiffened. Very faintly, in the distance, came the *whomp-whomp* sound of helicopter blades.

"Chinook," said Mount. "Remember that sound from Vietnam." He got up. "Think we best be going," he said.

Franklin put the laptop in "Sleep" mode, closed its cover, unplugged it, and handed it, along with its electric charger set, to Sandra. He turned off the light in the storage bay, and he and Mount rolled down the metal door and locked it.

The big helicopter was clearly visible in the early dawn light as it approached from the southwest. By the time the three had driven out of the self-storage compound and onto Arlington Boulevard, the copter was already descending for a landing in the driving range parking lot.

"I think we have to go directly to Senator Kydd," said Sandra. "I don't see that we have any choice."

"How do we get to him?" Franklin asked. "Even if I had my wallet, I don't think I could swing a big enough contribution for his reelection campaign to get his attention."

"I suppose I could show up at his office on a bogus anthrax scare," Sandra suggested unenthusiastically.

"Don't think you need to do any of that," said Mount softly. "Bright and early, fine summer morning, Senate not in session, only one place Senator Richard Kydd going to be."

Mount steered the big car north across the Potomac toward the Bethesda, Maryland, home of the Washington National Country Club.

CHAPTER 18

THE APPLE LAPTOP sat on the car's backseat, the little intermittently flashing green light on its back edge signaling that its core ROM was still operating. The pirate WiFi card that the Special Operations Squad had installed in the computer when they broke into Dumont's office made contact with each passing wireless access point as they drove by the high-technology office parks on the outskirts of the nation's capital.

It took twenty-three brief, separate, multimegabyte encounters with active router networks along the way to upload the entire contents of Hemmings Dumont's speech into the huge bank of Dell servers at C.I.A. headquarters in nearby Langley, Virginia, but the interruptions did provide a nice bonus. The route that the National Security Surveillance Subjects were taking up the Clara Barton Parkway and out toward River Road could be neatly mapped by the location of each succeeding broadcast of data.

The piercing, bat-like *twitter-tweet* of the Target Transmission Detector awakened the senior night duty officer on the Domestic Surveillance Desk from a light nap. Corbel Stanchion '89–"Baal" D.113–was a third-generation spook, and a tendency to doze on duty ran in the family. Wernher von Braun and the Nazi rocket scientists from Peenemünde had to wake up his grandfather Lintel from a deep snooze to arrange their surrender after Lintel had sampled the schnapps and schnitzel at the welcome picnic the O.S.S. had set up on the American side of the Elbe River in the spring of 1945; and Stanchion's father, Hustings, had slept through the shah of Iran's abdication speech in 1979, leading to his incarceration by Islamic student radicals for 444 days in Tehran.

Stanchion shook himself awake, ran a quick identity check on the coded prefix that preceded each binary data string in the narrowband WiFi broadcast from the Apple laptop, then pulled out his cell phone, dialed the number of the Sachem Club, and left a brief but urgent message.

He put away his cell phone and reached for the red phone. "Agent Stanchion, Domestic Operations," he barked into the handset. "Prepare Predator for immediate rollout and takeoff. Full war load. Launch authorization Oscar Kilo, Capital Area flyover clearance code 'Friendly Ghost.'"

The door on a squat, nondescript hangar at Andrews Air Force Base slid open, and a pair of flight mechanics wheeled the weird-looking, pilotless drone out onto a short stretch of unlighted runway.

As one of the plane handlers removed the safety lanyards from the warheads of the two Hellfire missiles that hung from the ungainly craft's stubby wings, the other ground crewman pressed the ignition button at the rear of the fuselage, just below its upside-down V-shaped tail fin.

"Cleared for takeoff," he said, and the two technicians dogtrotted back to the hangar together as the rear-mounted propeller spun into life. The robot aircraft rolled forward and taxied down the tarmac. With a low-pitched whine, it lifted off into the dawn sky and headed north across the Potomac toward the Maryland suburbs, briefly crossing ten thousand feet below the flight path of Air

Force Two, which was on course for its final approach to Andrews.

Agent Stanchion walked over to the alcove that held the remote-control cockpit and took a seat in front of the Virtual Pilot Guidance Display. He activated the onboard cameras, and a television monitor flickered on, showing a view of the south bank of the Potomac from 5,500 feet. He activated the WiFi Signal Homing Beacon, and as the drone crossed into Maryland, he gently rested his hand on the joystick, turned off the autopilot, and flipped the toggle switch marked ARM MISSILES.

Party time.

CHAPTER 19

THE SUN HAD just risen above the treetops as Mount turned off River Road and drove through the stately stone gates of the capital's most prestigious golf club. At the top of a hill, the baronial clubhouse of the Washington National Country Club loomed over the lush, impeccably groomed grounds, but halfway up the magnolia-lined drive, Mount turned off onto a side road marked by a discreet sign that read CADDY YARD.

He drove past several low, green-painted maintenance sheds and into a small parking area, screened by thick hedges, that held a motley assortment of battered high-mileage sedans with mismatched tires and Florida license plates.

Even though the first tee time of the morning was nearly an hour away, a couple of dozen mostly middle-aged, mostly black caddies, all of them already dressed in the club's distinctive white jumpsuits, were sitting on benches on the porch of the trim, shingled cabin that served as a caddyshack, drinking coffee and smoking.

Mount parked the Cadillac at the far end of the nearly full lot. "I'll see who's on the senator's bag today," he said, and headed over to the caddymaster's office.

Franklin and Sandra got out of the car and stretched.

"God, I'm beat," said Sandra, rubbing her eyes.

"Add dazed and confused," said Franklin, reaching back into the car for the Apple laptop. "I don't think I'll forget that stupid clue, but you never know," he said.

"There once was a dandy called doodle," said Sandra wearily.

"Let's get some air," said Franklin, and he and Sandra slipped through a small gap in the hedge and emerged at the edge of a sweeping, immaculately groomed emerald green fairway.

"Now I know why Congress never gets anything done," said Franklin, taking in the spectacular view.

Sandra stopped short, cocked an ear toward the sky, and held up a hand. "Hear that?" she asked.

Franklin stood still and listened intently. In the distance, he could barely make out the whine of a propeller-driven aircraft. "It's only a plane."

Sandra shook her head. "The entire airspace within the Capital Beltway is strictly off-limits to all civil aviation," she declared. The whine was growing louder.

Suddenly, with a sharp crackle of crushed underbrush, an electric golf cart shot out of the woods near the tee box of the long, meandering golf hole and bore down on them at full speed.

Sandra and Franklin instinctively turned and began to run back toward the caddyshack, but just at that moment, a second golf cart drove out from a row of trees on their side of the fairway and neatly cut them off.

Dexter Tollhouse, in lime green pants and a pink Lacoste polo shirt, stopped the cart directly in front of them, blocking their path. In the seat next to him, humming "Feelings" and lazily waving a sterling silver .38-caliber Tiffany Saturday evening special in their direction, sat Newell Banister.

"Professor Franklin, Ms. Damsel." Tollhouse smirked. "Just a twosome today? Mind if we play through?"

He dismounted from the cart and went up to Franklin. "I'm sorry, but electronic devices are prohibited on club property," he said smarmily. "I'm afraid I'll have to confiscate that laptop."

Franklin slipped the computer carrying case off his shoulder and started to hand it to Tollhouse, but the pudgy Bonesman held up a hand.

"Take it out of the case, please," he said. "We don't want any surprises."

Franklin did as he was told. As he slid the iBook out of its compartment in the carrying bag, he noticed for the first time the little aerial protruding from the edge of a credit card–size accessory chip inserted in the PCMCIA slot on the rear edge of the keyboard.

Tollhouse took the laptop and dropped it in the accessory basket behind the cart's rear seat.

The second golf cart pulled up. Merritt Parkway sat at the wheel, smoking a huge cigar, and Sterling Forest cradled a custom-made Purdy Doeblaster double-barreled shotgun.

Tollhouse reached into a pocket of the huge leather golf bag on the back of his cart and pulled out his pitchpipe blowgun and a flat metal box, from which he removed a dart. He delicately loaded it into the weapon's muzzle and signaled to the rest of the quartet. They immediately began singing a rousing version of "So Long, It's Been Good to Know You."

Sandra's eyes widened. "It was you!" she hissed. "You killed my uncle, you fat, smug, po-faced son of a bitch!" Sandra lunged at Tollhouse, but Franklin grabbed her by the waist and held her.

"Temper, temper," Tollhouse cooed nastily. "This should calm you down, my dear," he added, putting the blowgun to his lips. His cheeks puffed out, but just as he was about to exhale, a golf ball struck him on the side of his head, about an inch above his left ear, and the dart whizzed harmlessly into the trunk of a nearby tree.

A second ball hit Parkway's shoulder, and he dropped the pistol. Two hit Forest, and his shotgun discharged, blowing a large hole in the thick plastic roof of his cart. In rapid succession, one after the other, the balls rained down in a merciless fusillade.

Tollhouse jumped back in his cart and drove off, with Parkway and Forest following close behind.

A hundred yards away, Vernon Mount was swinging almost continuously at a long line of range balls scattered from an overturned wire basket. He paused as the Deathenpoofs fled down the fairway, then strolled over, twirling his 5-iron.

"Always liked the punch shot," he said.

"I'm glad you decided to work on your short game," said Franklin soberly.

"Ran into a friend of mine in the parking lot, name of Lou Moon," said Mount. "Works over at the Sachem Club, where those gentlemen are staying. They paid him to chauffeur them out here. Lou said they had guns in their bags. Didn't much like the sound of that."

"We owe Mr. Moon a lot," said Sandra.

"You're not the only one. Told me to invest in Calloway stock at the start, got me out at the top." He smiled. "I *own* that driving range."

As the Predator swooped low over the back nine of Washington National, Stanchion adjusted the focal length of the videocamera. The little red laser dot of the Vector Locator tuned to the 802.11g protocol signal of the Apple laptop's AirPort card was fixed directly on the rear of one of the two golf carts speeding down the center of the club's signature par-5, fourteenth hole.

Stanchion pulled lightly on the joystick, and the Predator turned left, descended to one hundred feet, and slowed to forty-five miles per hour as it took up a firing position behind the speeding carts.

"Hasta la vista," Stanchion murmured as he pressed both triggers.

The two Hellfire missiles streaked toward their aiming points. Tollhouse must have heard the rocket motors ignite. A split second before the first missile hit, he turned and looked back up into the sky.

The high-resolution camera caught his face in full close-up, and Stanchion instantly recognized the familiar features of his fellow Bonesman, one of the society's most distinguished Patriarchs. He gave the joystick a violent yank, and the Predator climbed steeply, but it was too late. The armor-piercing rockets, which were originally designed to destroy forty-ton Soviet-era T-72 main battle tanks, slammed into the flimsy golf carts.

Oopsy-daisy.

There was a pair of brief bright flashes, followed by two dull *whumps*, and the golf carts and their occupants simply ceased to exist, leaving behind nothing more than a thick pall of oily smoke, a few scraps of red-hot metal, and a pair of large, side-by-side black scorch marks on the pristine turf.

Mount whistled in admiration. "Now that right there

is one mighty effective way to deal with slow play on the golf course," he said approvingly.

Franklin and Sandra stood in stunned silence. A few infinitesimal pieces of debris rained down nearby and settled on the grass. Something caught Franklin's eye. He reached down and picked it up.

It was a ragged, two-inch-square piece of pink cloth with a little green crocodile in its center.

Mount turned to Sandra. "I got word to Senator Kydd," he said. "He's up on the practice putting green. Says he's looking forward to meeting Mr. Dumont's niece."

CHAPTER 20

THE VICE PRESIDENT'S Gulfstream taxied to a stop at the heavily guarded Executive Branch Transit Terminal at Andrews Air Force Base. Dick Cheney released the buckle on his seat belt and reached for his briefcase. The steward immediately materialized in the aisle.

"Sir, we do ask that for your own safety and that of the passengers traveling with you, you remain seated until we come to a full stop at the gate," the steward said curtly.

Cheney sighed and sat back and crossed his legs.

"Flight attendant, prepare for arrival and cross-check," said the steward, speaking into the right-hand sleeve of his jacket.

He looked up. "It is now safe to move about the cabin. But please exercise caution when retrieving personal items from the overhead bins—they may have shifted during flight and could fall out, causing injuries."

Cheney got up and headed for the exit. "Have a nice day in the Washington area or wherever your final destination may be," the steward trilled brightly.

The vice president's limousine was parked less than ten feet from the narrow flight of aluminum steps that had folded down from the business jet's fuselage. A uniformed air force officer saluted and opened the rear passenger door. Cheney gave him a halfhearted Boy Scout salute and got in. The stretch Continental already had a passenger.

"Good flight?" asked Don Rumsfeld.

"It sucked," said Cheney sourly.

Rumsfeld folded his arms. "Is flying a pain?" he asked in his trademark rhetorical style as the car headed out on Curtis LeMay Boulevard toward Pennsylvania Avenue. "Why, yes, it is. Is there anything we can do about it? Well, frankly, no, there isn't much we can do about it. It's the price we pay to enjoy freedom of movement. If we're not willing to pay that price, then my goodness, we might just as well stay home."

Cheney smiled wanly. "Thanks for coming, Don."

"Was I happy to come? You bet I was," said Rumsfeld animatedly. "Did it involve some inconvenience? Of course it did. But sometimes we have to sacrifice a little bit of comfort to accomplish what we set out to do."

Cheney groaned. "Don, we have a problem."

Rumsfeld thought this over. "Dick, there are problems that have solutions, and once we find those solutions, they cease to be problems. They become ex-problems. They are effectively deproblemized, and their capacity for problemization is sharply degraded. And then there are problems that have no apparent solution. They exhibit maximum problemisticity. They are thorny, they are knotty. They are problematic problems." He leaned forward. "Is this a problematic problem?"

Cheney nodded. "This is problemacious in the extreme. This is problemetatastical."

Rumsfeld shrugged. "I'm all ears."

Cheney looked out the window at the towering tail of Air Force One protruding from a maintenance hangar that would easily cover two city blocks. Out of the corner of his eye, he saw a Predator come in for a landing.

Somebody's on the ball.

He turned and looked directly at Rumsfeld. "I think we're going to lose the election."

Rumsfeld snorted. "Give me three reasons why."

"The economy is in the toilet, the war in Iraq is a disaster, and nobody trusts us on terrorism."

Rumsfeld narrowed his eyes. "Those aren't reasons, those are conditions. Conditions change. They're transient. They're conditional. Reasons are unconditional. Give me a reason."

"The President is a nitwit," said Cheney matter-of-factly.

Rumsfeld exhaled in audible relief. "Dick, we *know* the President is a nitwit. This is not new news. This is old, old news. Of course he's a nitwit. But he's *our* nitwit. My golly, he'd have to be a nitwit to let us run things."

Cheney glared at him.

"Just kidding," said Rumsfeld quickly. "Look, Dick, is it a bad thing that the President is a nitwit? No, it isn't. It is a good thing. Why? Because it's his greatest strength. This is a nation of nitwits. They love this guy. That's why they elected him. He's just like them. He's average. He's ordinary. He doesn't have original thoughts. He doesn't speak in complete sentences. He can't balance a checkbook. He hates to wait. He wants his cheeseburger now. He's a bit of a bully, and a bit of a coward, and he's shallow, and he's mean, and when he screws up, he does what any red-blooded American would do—he blames it on somebody else and moves on."

The cell phone in Cheney's pocket rang, playing the first few notes of "The Ride of the Valkyries." He looked at the caller ID. It read "41."

"Good morning, Mr. President," said Cheney genially. "How's the weather up there in Maine?" His expression darkened. "Yes, sir, I'm sitting down."

As he listened to the report from George Bush Senior, what little color there actually was in his face drained completely away. "Yes, sir, it sure is a pretty pickle," he said. "You have a nice day, too, sir."

Cheney snapped the phone shut. "We no longer have a problem—now we have real trouble—big-time!" He summarized for Rumsfeld the deeply disturbing message from the President's father.

It didn't happen often, but Rumsfeld was at a loss for words. "Judas Priest," he finally managed to croak.

CHAPTER 21

FRANKLIN LED THE way as he, Mount, and Sandra headed back through the hedge along the side of the fairway toward the caddyshack parking lot. He had barely emerged from the wall of privet when he did an about-face and pushed Sandra and Mount back out onto the course.

It had taken him only a moment to register the government Ford with the JUST MARRIED sign and the crepe paper and a string of tin cans and boots tied to its rear bumper and to catch a glimpse of Agent Fine barking answers at a group of baffled caddies on the porch.

"It's the Homeland Security Agents," Franklin whispered.

Sandra looked dumbstruck. "How did they find us?"

"The laptop had a wireless card," said Franklin. "I must have missed it in that dark storage room. I saw it when I gave it to that glee club dickhead. They've been tracking us from the start."

"Wait here," said Mount, and he disappeared through the hedge.

"Fine and Dandy," said Franklin bitterly. "It'll be a real feather in their cap if they nail us."

Sandra looked as if she'd just won the lottery. "Hoowee," she cried, then quickly put a hand over her mouth. "You know, Professor," she continued in a whisper, "you really have a knack for the code-breaking business."

Franklin stared at her blankly.

"Yankee Doodle went to town, riding on a pony, stuck a feather in his cap—" she sang in a low voice.

"And called it macaroni," said Franklin, finishing the timeless colonial ditty.

"There once was a dandy called doodle, with a cap plume named after a noodle; that pasta's my address," Sandra recited, pausing momentarily as she tried to remember the rest.

"His nag's breed will access the fast mail that leads to the boodle," said Franklin.

"It's e-mail," said Sandra. "macaroni@fastmail.com."

"And the password is PONY," said Franklin. "Damn, I wish we'd figured that out before the Brooks Brothers got vaporized, along with our laptop."

"No problem," said Sandra. "We can access his e-mail from anywhere, even my cell phone."

At that moment, Mount reappeared carrying two golf bags, one over each shoulder, two pairs of caddy overalls, and two Washington National Country Club baseball-style hats.

"Your lucky day," he said slyly. "Got you both a loop."

Senator Richard Kydd had just missed his tenth consecutive four-foot practice putt on the club's enormous putting green when Mount, Franklin, and Sandra walked up. All three were carrying golf bags, and Franklin and Sandra had pulled the bills of their caps so low over their eyes, they could barely see.

Mount put down his bag and walked over to the silver-haired senator, who at the age of eighty-three still looked amazingly spry. He also looked amazingly pissed off.

"I think we might want to go back to that old bull's-eye putter, Senator," said Mount, eyeing with deep suspicion the strange hoop-headed club the senator was wielding.

Senator Kydd looked up. "Vernon," he said, his voice mellow with the practiced cadences of a lifetime of political oratory, "if I putt like this, I think I can say without fear of contradiction, I am not going to shoot my age—I am going to shoot my weight."

A few yards away from Kydd, Senator Christopher Dodd sank a twenty-foot, double-breaking, ridiculous snake of a putt. "Richard, esteemed colleague," he said cheerfully, "you can hand over your wallet right now."

Kydd scowled and walked off the green. Mount followed him and beckoned Sandra and Franklin over. They put down their golf bags and joined Mount. "Senator," he said quietly, "this is Mr. Dumont's niece Sandra Damsel and Professor William Franklin."

Kydd looked puzzled by the caddy outfits, but his demeanor immediately improved. With a showy flourish he kissed Sandra's hand. "And how is your uncle, Miss Damsel? I'm long overdue for a historical discussion with that most distinguished scholar."

"He's dead, Senator," said Sandra flatly. "He was murdered last night in the Smithsonian."

Kydd's face froze. "The documents?"

"They are real. And we think they're still safe."

Kydd turned to Franklin. "*The* Professor Franklin, author of *The Kabbalah Shibboleth?*" he asked.

"Er, yes, sir," said Franklin.

"Hell of a read," said Kydd. "Any of it true?"

"Um, some of it is fairly unfallacious," said Franklin unconvincingly.

"And your choice of haberdashery?" asked Kydd, arching his eyebrows. "I must warn you, caddying is a very demanding profession."

"There are a couple of Homeland Security agents on the club grounds," said Sandra, seeing no choice but to trust the veteran senator. "There's a bogus National Security warrant out for us—they think we know where those documents are."

"Patriot Act," said Kydd, practically spitting out the words in disgust. "Despot Act is more like it."

He waved at a congressional aide, and the young, preppy-looking legislative assistant hurried over.

"Howard, be a good lad and bring the car around," said Kydd. "Miss Damsel, Professor Franklin, and I are going to my Capitol office."

The assistant gave Sandra and Franklin a brief, startled look, then headed for the valet parking area. Once he was out of sight, he reached into his jacket pocket, pulled out a cell phone, and dialed a Washington number.

Kydd took the space-age putter, dropped it in a nearby litter basket, then walked over to Senator Dodd.

"Alas, Christopher, duty calls," he said, not sounding terribly distressed. "No game today, I fear."

"Now just a minute, Richard," Dodd protested. "You can't just call off a match because you've got the yips."

"I assure you, this is a matter of great urgency," said Kydd. Something in his voice gave Dodd the distinct impression that for once, one of the world's great bullshit artists was not wielding his traditional silver shovel.

"It better be a matter of life and death," said Dodd.

"Oh, it is far more serious than that," said Kydd gravely. "On this hinges the very survival of the Republic."

Senator Kydd's surprisingly modest Lincoln Town Car pulled up with his aide at the wheel. The only sign of the distinction of its owner was the set of Maryland plates with a simple number "1" in the middle.

Mount opened the rear door, and Senator Kydd motioned Sandra into the backseat, then followed her. Franklin got in the front seat. Mount leaned into the car. "You sure have been a fun couple," he said, "but I think from now on I'll stick to golf." He gave Senator Kydd a respectful salute and shut the door.

Sandra blew him a kiss, and he strolled away.

"Traffic's going to be murder this time of the morning,

Senator," said Howie Cheatham as he steered the Lincoln down the club driveway.

"Take the Kyddway," said Kydd, "I'd be honored to have the opportunity to point out a few of my modest achievements to my guests."

In truth, very few people other than Senator Richard Kydd were aware that the broad, multilane expressway that circled the Washington metropolitan area was not named the Beltway—it was the Richard Kydd Capital District Peripheral Highway. Of course, he was the only person who ever referred to it as the Kyddway, but the eight-term senator from Maryland didn't care. He hadn't spent five decades mastering the Senate's arcane appropriations process just to get his name on things. No, what mattered to him was obtaining thousands upon thousands of well-paid government jobs for his historic but minor and easily overlooked home state.

As the Lincoln swept through this now remarkably prosperous swath of Montgomery County, Kydd happily pointed out to his captive audience the clusters of official buildings scattered through the landscape: the Office of Pet Statistics, the Interstate Motto Commission, the Job Duplication Agency, the Jargon Review Board, the Federal

Lost Application Administration, the Busy-Signal Corps, the Internal Hyphenation Service, and the National Center for Needless Expenditure.

Kydd soon realized that Sandra and Franklin were not actually speechless at his accomplishments. They were, in fact, fast asleep.

He smiled sadly. *Let them sleep. The whole country is asleep. And if it doesn't wake up very soon, it is headed for an unimaginable nightmare.*

CHAPTER 22

THE DAILY PRAYER breakfast in the large third-floor conference room of the somber gray Department of Justice building overlooking Constitution Avenue always began at eight o'clock sharp.

The last stragglers hastened past the untouched buffet of hot-cross buns and sardines, a meager and revolting spread dictated by Attorney General Ashcroft's strict reading of the Gospels' accounts of the feeding of loaves and fishes to the multitudes.

Ashcroft sat at the head of the heavy government-issue conference table, his hand on a well-thumbed Bible. Most of the senior Justice Department officials were present, and the few who weren't were headed for early retirement, whether they knew it or not.

The young federal prosecutor who had handled the first successful death penalty prosecution of an autistic child closed the door, and the nation's top law enforcement officer gestured to two visitors seated across from each other in places of honor at the center of each side of the table. One was a jowly, dog-faced, middle-aged man in Sansabelt slacks and a double-knit sports jacket. The other was a man of about seventy, expensively dressed in a well-tailored suit, with crinkly eyes and perfect teeth.

"Brethren," Ashcroft intoned, "we are very honored to have with us today to lead us in prayer two of America's greatest preachers and moral leaders, Reverend Jordy Weevil and Reverend Pud Buggerson."

Weevil went first. "Oh, Lord," he crooned in a backwoods Georgia twang, "we beseech you to strike down the homosexuals who seek to defile the holy sacrament of matrimony. Turn their vile willies into tiny pillars of salt, cause their testicles to erupt in pustulant boils, send bolts of purgatorial lightning up their foul, sodomized fundaments, and cast them into bottomless pools of hot, stinking vomit."

"Amen," Ashcroft thundered approvingly.

Buggerson frowned. Weevil had stolen his sermon on gay weddings, practically verbatim, from last Sunday's *Godly Hour of Christian Hate* radio broadcast. *That redneck turd.*

Oh, well, go with the old standby. "Oh, Lord," he inveighed in an upper-class, faintly Virginian accent, "we call upon you to send a gigantic flaming comet to strike Hollywood and utterly decimate and incinerate the godless dwellings of the merchants of filth and slime. Pierce their lustful eyeballs with jets of purifying flame, melt their lip studs and nose rings until the very flesh burns off their faces, boil them alive in their hot tubs so that their skin bursts and coarse fatty juices flow forth like grease from a split sausage casing. But spare Mel Gibson," he quickly added.

"Amen," Ashcroft intoned.

Just then the door opened, and a federal marshal stepped partway into the room.

"We're at prayer," Ashcroft exclaimed angrily.

"I'm sorry, General," said the lawman, "but we just got some urgent intelligence on Operation Gadarene Swine. Professor Franklin and Agent Sandra Damsel are on their way to the Capitol with Senator Richard Kydd."

Ashcroft rose abruptly from his seat and addressed the congregants.

"The hour for prayer is over," he said solemnly. "Now it is time for the terrible swift sword." He turned and left the room.

"Praise God," said Buggerson.

"Bust their ever-lovin' balls," said Weevil.

CHAPTER 23

AS CHEATHAM EXITED onto the Baltimore-Washington Parkway, the motion of the tight turn jolted Sandra awake.

She blinked a few times. "I'm sorry, Senator," she said a little woozily. "We had a very long night."

Kydd patted her hand in a grandfatherly way. "You are not the first person who has fallen asleep during one of my speeches," he said, "and I am quite sure you will not be the last."

Franklin stirred at the sound of their voices and looked out the windshield. Off in the distance, rising through the haze, he could just make out the gleaming dome of the U.S. Capitol.

"What a weird dream," he said. "I get picked up at my hotel by a couple of federal agents, I'm taken to a museum where there's a dead guy on the floor, I escape in a bird costume, and I follow a trail of really dopey clues, and then I get mugged in a driving range parking lot, and after that I go to a storage room to see the dead guy from the museum give a show-and-tell video about some two-hundred-year-old documents that are going to turn this town upside down, and then a barbershop quartet of homicidal Ivy League fruitcakes in a golf cart tries to kill me with a blowgun, but a robot plane blows them to smithereens."

"It wasn't a dream," said Sandra.

"Somehow I just knew you were going to say that," said Franklin as the Lincoln suddenly swerved.

"Sorry, Senator," said Cheatham. "Dodging a pothole."

Kydd looked at Sandra intently. "Dumont actually had the documents?"

Sandra nodded. "They looked real. I don't believe he would have been murdered for a figment of his imagination, or that he would have gone to so much trouble to create such an elaborate maze of clues to protect a forgery." She pulled out a Samsung cell phone. "We have one last clue," she remembered suddenly.

She called up the menu, selected Wireless Web, and

punched in macaroni@fastmail.com. When the password dialog box flashed on the screen, she entered P-O-N-Y. There was a brief pause as the server downloaded messages. There were two. She clicked on the first.

It was a bewildering string of seemingly random letters and numbers:

PN6231. S497866 1990 817'.5407–dc20 90-53150

Franklin saw a small notepad and pen in the little storage compartment between the two front seats. "May I?" he said to Cheatham.

"Of course," said Cheatham. Franklin took the pad, and as Sandra repeated the message, this time more slowly, he wrote it down. He tore off the scrap of paper. It had the logo of the Yale Club of New York on it.

"What on earth is it?" Sandra wondered aloud.

Kydd chuckled. "We know what it is, don't we, Howard?"

"So do I," said Franklin. "It's a Library of Congress catalog number for a specific book."

"They do have a most idiosyncratic system," said Kydd. He looked at his watch. "They won't open for another hour. Time to get you some breakfast."

As the car drove up Independence Avenue toward the Capitol building, Sandra clicked on the second message.

P.S. YOU'RE GETTING WARMER!

CHAPTER 24

QUICK BROWN FOX waited until all the other passengers got off the bus from New Haven, then picked up the satchel with the skull of Geronimo and the ceremonial medicine stick, made his way down the aisle, and took a deep breath of fresh air as he disembarked. Buses were for suckers.

He went over to a map of the Capitol district mounted on a nearby wall and located the Smithsonian. It was over a mile away, but he was stiff from the six-hour ride and he welcomed the opportunity to stretch his legs.

He slung the bag over his shoulder and headed toward

the Mall. The head of the great Apache warrior was on its way home.

The vice president's limousine pulled into Executive Avenue and came to a stop in front of the West Wing of the White House. A Marine guard in dress uniform opened the rear door, then escorted Cheney and Rumsfeld to the front door of the Executive Mansion, opened it, and saluted.

As Lance Corporal Gus "Goody" Gumdropcyz resumed his position on the front steps, his lips silently formed the *m, th, f, k,* and *r* phonemes of a popular military epithet.

What a sorry-ass pair of gomers. Cheech and Chong could have done a better job of running the war in Iraq.

"I'll see you downstairs in about an hour," said Cheney. Rumsfeld nodded and headed for the elevator that would take him to the bombproof command center deep beneath the White House.

Cheney followed a thickly carpeted corridor that led to the Oval Office. He checked his watch: 8:55. Right on time.

Chief of Staff Andy Card was standing just outside the

Oval Office door. "Good morning, Mr. Vice President," he said. "They're waiting for you."

Cheney smiled his tight little smile and walked into the most famous office in the world.

President George W. Bush was leaning back in his chair with his feet propped up on his desk, almost knocking over a sign that read:

THE BUCK STOPS HERE–
AND SO FAR IN THIS FUND-RAISING SEASON
200 MILLION BUCKS HAVE STOPPED HERE!

On a pair of facing couches a short distance away sat Representative Tom DeLay, Senate majority leader Bill Frist, and Republican Party leader Marc Racicot. In one of two wing chairs closer to the President's desk sat senior White House political adviser Karl Rove. Cheney took a seat in the other one.

"Hey, Ricardo," said Bush breezily. "Welcome back from Hernando's Hideaway!"

"Good to be back, Mr. President," said Cheney, forcing himself to smile at the lame gag. He hated Bush's habit of giving everyone a nickname. It was juvenile and more than once had given serious offense to the recipients of the asinine monikers. For instance, there was the time Bush had addressed Pope John Paul II as "Mumbles" during what was supposed to be an hour-long audience at the Vatican that was quickly cut short by the peeved pontiff.

Equally memorable had been the formal after-dinner speech at the G-8 conference last year when he had introduced President Jacques Chirac of France as "my old friend Pepé Le Pew," and the time he welcomed Chancellor Gerhard Schröder of Germany to the White House with a somewhat undiplomatic Nazi salute and a cry of "Schultz!" in a bad imitation of Colonel Klink from *Hogan's Heroes,* or last summer in Crawford when he greeted a startled and not very amused Prime Minister Junichiro Koizumi of Japan by holding his arms straight out, making a sort of propeller noise, and shouting, "Hit the deck—kamikaze at two o'clock!"

"OK, let's get this show on the road," said the President. "Veepster, what's the skinny on the election?"

Cheney looked glum. "Mr. President, I'll be blunt. If we don't get our rear ends in gear, we're headed for defeat in November."

Bush's face darkened. "I want a game plan," he snapped.

Karl Rove spoke up. "Mr. President, we need more wedge issues," he said. "Our constitutional amendment to ban gay marriage is a good start, but we need to go further. I'd like us to also propose a ban on gay funerals—and no mealy-mouthed 'civil burial' or 'gay rites' exceptions. A queer dies, he goes to the glue factory, and that's that."

"Wouldn't want to lick that envelope," said Marc Racicot to general laughter.

"Great idea, Karl," Bush exclaimed. "And you know, we could get more mileage out of the whole abortion thing, too. Let's lower the legal age for just about everything to zero, and give fetuses the right to vote and own a gun."

DeLay and Frist exchanged nervous glances.

"Think about it," Bush went on, clearly warming to the concept. "No embryo in its right mind is going to vote for a pro-choice candidate, and if the mom tries to terminate the pregnancy and goes to one of those abortion clinics, why, the little feller can blow that butcher's head off!"

There was a moment of stunned silence, which Tom DeLay broke. "Um, Mr. President, I think we could use more tax relief. Here's a new angle I've been working on with Grover Norquist. What do you say that instead of taxing folks on what they earn or save, we tax them on what they *owe*. I mean, we've got about four trillion dollars in household debt in this country, so we're talking real money here, and with a debt tax, as I call it, we'd be taking revenue from a bunch of deadbeats instead of productive entrepreneurs and businesspeople."

"I think you've got something there, Tom," said Senator Frist. "Now if I can just put my two cents in—which is one cent more than I paid in taxes this year, thanks to one very smart accountant—speaking as a medical man, we could set it up so if someone couldn't pay what they owe on what they owe, they could cough up a kidney or a piece of liver or something along those lines."

"Can't we just invade somebody?" Bush interjected. "How about North Korea? I hate those guys."

Cheney cleared his throat. "Mr. President, we're stretched pretty thin what with Iraq and Afghanistan. And North Korea is no pushover."

"Well, what about East Korea," said Bush petulantly. "Or one of those other 'stans—you know, like Parmestan, or Umbrellastan, or Spicandspanistan."

"Maybe after the election, Mr. President," said Cheney, surreptitiously popping a heart pill into his mouth.

Bush looked at his watch impatiently and got to his feet. Everyone else in the room immediately rose. "Look, enough beating around the, er, thing you beat around," said Bush. "I want to see some fighting spirit. Give me a *V*!" he called out, punching the air with his right hand.

"V," came the not very lusty chant.

"Give me an *I*!" said Bush a little louder.

"I," the group replied.

"Give me a *C*!" said Bush.

"C," the five top-level officials repeated.

"Give me a *K*!" said Bush.

"K?" came the somewhat puzzled echo.

"Give me a *T*!"

"T."

"Give me a *U*!"

"U?"

"Give me an *R*!"

"R."

"Give me an *E*!"

"E?"

"Give me a *Y*!"

"Y."

"What does it spell?"

There was another awkward silence.

"Vickshuree?" Racicot ventured.

"Louder!" Bush insisted.

"Vickshuree!" they all cried.

"Yay," Bush whooped. "Now let's all get out there and pull together. Remember," he added earnestly, "there is no *I* in *Team*." The President paused for a moment. "Is there?"

CHAPTER 25

CHEATHAM LEFT Senator Kydd, Sandra, and Franklin at the restricted Capitol entrance reserved for members of Congress and their guests, and then drove off to park the car in the garage of the Russell Senate Office Building.

Security around the Capitol was tight, but nobody felt like challenging the dean of the United States Senate, and the three passed unhampered into the monumental stone structure. They crossed under the ornate, soaring Rotunda, and Kydd led the way down a corridor to a series of private offices on the west side of the huge building reserved for the most senior legislators.

Kydd occupied the most coveted suite of rooms in the

Capitol, a grandiose corner layout with two fireplaces, twenty-foot-high ceilings, and a wide balcony overlooking the Mall. The tall oak doors to the office's reception area were open, and Sandra and Franklin exchanged hungry glances as they smelled the unmistakable aroma of freshly brewed coffee and the mouthwatering odors of a multi-course hot breakfast.

"Well, I wonder what fine group of public-spirited businessmen is gracing us with their presence today," Kydd said cheerfully. He ushered them into a cavernous vestibule where a full buffet was being served by white-jacketed chefs to a handful of Senate committee staffers.

A placard mounted on a folding wooden easel read *National Association of Manufacturers of Defective and Unsafe Products,* and an oily public relations representative with a thick pompadour stood by the door acting as a greeter.

"Senator Kydd," he burbled, holding out his hand. "Delighted you could stop by. Hale Hardy, of the N.A.M.D.U.P. We certainly do appreciate your giving us the opportunity to share with your staff our views on this pending legislation mandating a virtually unlimited thirty-day warranty period for consumer goods and an increase in the already astronomical five-hundred-dollar cap on damages to a truly confiscatory thousand dollars."

Kydd shook Hardy's hand, then made a show of counting his fingers. He turned to Sandra and Franklin. "Dig in," he said, pointing to the buffet.

Dig in they did. Sandra had the eggs Benedict. Franklin had the corned beef hash with poached egg. They both had the smoked salmon.

Kydd went over to the desk of his stupefyingly rude and remarkably potty-mouthed secretary, "Horrible Hilda" Basilisk, a 225-pound former professional lady wrestler who dedicated herself enthusiastically to the task of shielding the senator from the virtually nonstop importunings of the capital's army of highly paid lobbyists.

"Want me to break a chair over his head?" she inquired eagerly, motioning to Hardy, who was glad-handing the chief counsel of the Standing Subcommittee on Statutory Loopholes.

"Let's wait until my guests finish breakfast," said Kydd. "Send them in when they've eaten their fill." He went into his private chambers and closed the door.

He walked over to the window and looked out on the bright, sunlit Mall. In the distance, the simple limestone shaft of the Washington Monument almost glowed in the morning light.

Two thousand years ago, Cicero must have once stood in a place like this, looking out over the Forum, fearing for his Republic as I fear for mine.

There was a knock on the door and Sandra and Franklin came in. Kydd went over to his desk, took out a laminated plastic card, and handed it to Sandra. "This is my senatorial Library of Congress pass. It will give you access to the stacks where the volumes are actually stored." He reached into another compartment in the drawer, slipped out a business card, and handed that over, too. "My private phone number," he said.

He walked over to the room's intricately carved marble fireplace, put a hand on the mantel, and struck a senatorial pose. "I hardly dare to hope that those documents truly exist, but if they do, you must find them. The shock of their disquieting revelations may be the only thing that will prevent this abominable administration from prevailing in the elections.

"Two millennia ago, through hereditary succession, another republic fell into the hands of a vain and foolish boy emperor. Its legions, in which the sons of the prosperous no longer served, were sent to fight and die in fruitless campaigns in hostile lands. Its treasury was depleted, its commerce ruined, its liberties transgressed. The amity and respect of longtime allies were squandered in an unconscionable display of arrogance, greed, and fanaticism. Its citizenry paid no heed. They cared only for comfort and spectacle. They fell prey to demagogues and charlatans. They awoke one day to tyranny, but by then it was too late.

"*Qui historiam non cognoscit, cursum iterabit.*" He sighed.

"Those who do not study history are condemned to repeat it," Franklin translated.

"You know Latin," said the senator approvingly.

"I took it in high school, but I had to basically relearn it when I was researching *The Pompeii Perplexity.*"

"A real page-turner," said Senator Kydd. "But I am not entirely sure I accept your hypothesis that the eruption of Vesuvius was triggered by renegade Roman military engineers working in a secret subterranean foundry on an experimental atomic catapult."

"Well, obviously there were some places where I was forced to rely on conjecture—"

The intercom on Kydd's desk buzzed. "Couple of dirtballs named Fine and Dandy from the Department of Homeland Security to see you, Senator," said Hilda through the speaker.

"See that they get some breakfast—I'll meet with them in due course."

He went over to a small door to the right of the fireplace and opened it, revealing a circular cast-iron stair that led down to the Capitol's lower level.

"My predecessors used it for assignations," he said. "Alas, I am well past the age when I can engage in such pursuits. Godspeed."

Sandra kissed him lightly on the cheek, and she and Franklin clattered down the metal steps.

The intercom buzzed again. "Senator, Attorney General Ashcroft is on the line. The scumbag insists on talking to you immediately."

"Give him an evasive answer," said Kydd in an imitation of W. C. Fields that Franklin would have envied. "Tell him to go fuck himself."

Hale Hardy came over to Fine and Dandy. "So you're from Homeland Security—couldn't help overhearing. Hardy's the name, product liability's the game," he said, extending a hand, which each of the agents shook.

"You know," he said, "we in the litigation suppression industry are always on the lookout for experienced government personnel interested in a rewarding career in the private sector. We've got openings in a number of fields: witness intimidation, incriminating personal information collection, document modification, evidence disposal, you name it. The pay is excellent."

He handed the pair a couple of glossy brochures.

"Well, how much are we talking about here?" Fine inquired, sounding interested.

"Starting pay for someone with, say, twenty years' service in law enforcement at the federal level is $145,000."

Fine whistled. "Wow," he said, "that's serious money."

"Much travel?" asked Dandy.

"Some," Handy conceded. "But all first-class, with a generous expense account."

As Fine and Dandy examined the printed material, Cheatham came in and sat down at his desk in the far corner of the room. He took out the notepad he had removed from the car and rubbed a soft pencil over the top sheet. The pen Franklin had used to write down the catalog number from the e-mail Sandra had retrieved on her cell phone had left a clear impression in the paper, and the numbers and letters were easily legible.

He reached into the bottom drawer of the desk and took out a flat oilskin packet. He opened his wallet and made sure he had his congressional aide's library stack pass. He walked toward the door.

"Hold it right there, pal," said Fine. "Our orders are that no one leaves this office."

"Er, I have to go get my teeth cleaned or my driver's license renewed, I can't remember which," Cheatham stammered.

"I smell a rat," said Dandy.

"It sounds fishy all right," Fine agreed.

Hilda got up from her desk, walked over, grabbed each of them by the back of his neck, and slammed their foreheads together. The two agents' skulls collided with a sickening *fonk*, and they slumped to the floor.

"Beat it, asshole," she said to Cheatham, who made a speedy exit.

CHAPTER 26

CHENEY'S HEAD was still spinning from the President's pep rally as he entered the elevator that connected the White House offices with the Presidential Emergency Operations Center almost two hundred feet below ground level.

He didn't relish the prospect of reporting to the Elders on the sorry state of the reelection effort. Bush's infatuation with Karl Rove was a total mystery to him. He had basically run a losing campaign in 2000, and he'd handled the famous Senate campaign of John Ashcroft, who had made history by being the first major political candidate in modern times to be defeated by a dead opponent.

He had no idea how Rove had gained a reputation as some kind of Machiavelli. Baloney. The man was a moron.

Cheney punched his ultrasecure code into the alphanumeric keypad that controlled access to the shelter.

The fourteen-letter code was easy to remember. It was his own private nickname for the President. As the entry was being verified, it briefly appeared on an LED readout display:

SPURIOUSGEORGE

A bell dinged, and the elevator descended rapidly.

The doors opened onto a low-ceilinged, fluorescent-lit war room filled with analysts watching banks of video monitors. There were live spy-satellite views of a variety of battlefields in Iraq and Afghanistan, as well as high-resolution close-up images of the Kremlin, the Chinese Communist Party headquarters at Zhongnanhai in Beijing, Kim Jong Il's fortress-like compound in Pyongyang, the government buildings in Tehran, and *New York Times* columnist Paul Krugman's house in Princeton, New Jersey.

Farther on, there was a separate bank of television sets tuned to the nation's hush-hush fiber optic network of cybernetically scrambled cable channels.

On the Cabal News Network, they were showing a pre-peat of tonight's blockbuster Larry King interview, conducted mostly in simian sign language, with Michael Jackson's chimp, Bobo, and his attorney, a fat, talkative, green-feathered macaw with a big beak, named Parrot L. Shapiro, who was representing the aggrieved ape in a ten-million-banana lawsuit accusing the troubled rock star of inappropriate monkey business at his Santa Ynez ranch.

Tomorrow's closing stock prices ran along the bottom of the screen. The market was headed for another down week.

Damn. He'd have to make a point to watch Wall Street Week in Preview, *the new program of interviews with inside traders, hosted by Louis Rukeyser's evil but extremely well-informed sister, Zoe.*

The next set over was tuned to Al Jibberjabba, the Arabic-language channel, which was broadcasting a subtitled rant by the hooded leader of the Palestinian militant organization Hummus, which had just extended its campaign of terror to Iraq, carrying out a spate of deadly bombings of falafel stands with booby-trapped bowls of bean dip.

Nearby, another television ran ESPN-VIP, which was showing a boxing match between the Abominable Snowman and Kleznog, the bug-eyed alien from the top-secret

U.F.O. lab at Area 51 in Nevada. On the next television after that were offerings from QT-TV, the government's Defense Shopping Network. They were offering a pair of Star Wars krypton lasers for $4,999,000, an absolute steal. Cheney was a big fan of the station. In fact, he'd just ordered a depleted-uranium hot tray for his wife Lynne's birthday.

The last screen in the line had the FOX Channel. They were already running Cheney's doctored footage of Senator John Kerry using a flaming American flag to set fire to a pile of Bibles. The news crawl at the bottom of the screen was the same one the public saw, but this special classified version had all the outright lies circled in red.

Cheney crossed the room to a spaceship-style metal door. He gave the ancient ritual knock first used almost five centuries earlier by the Court Barbers of Seville in the palace of the king of Spain:

SHAVE-AND-A-HAIRCUT, TWO BITS

The door hissed open to let him enter, then immediately slid shut behind him.

He surveyed the room. Every seat along the flanks of the black onyx conference table was taken. On the near side of the room sat Don Rumsfeld, Paul Wolfowitz, Doug

Feith, Scooter Libby, and Richard Perle. On the far side were David Rockefeller, Henry Kissinger, Queen Elizabeth, Alan Greenspan, Rupert Murdoch, and a Swiss banker in lederhosen and a green alpine hat.

Cheney took his seat at the head of the table, facing down its length to a vacant chair at the other end only a few feet away from the metal door of another elevator.

He laid a folder on the table and opened it. "I have some good news, and some bad news," he said, making eye contact with each member of his audience in turn.

"Leading with the good news, burying the bad news on page fifty," said Murdoch, his Australian accent giving an incongruous lilt to FOX's trademark verbless, participle-heavy narrative style.

"I do so hate *nuntius horribilis,*" said Queen Elizabeth, stroking the corgi in her lap.

"Vee vill decide vhat is good and vhat is bad, buttvipe," said Kissinger unpleasantly.

Greenspan seemed to agree, although as always, it was almost impossible to extract any actual meaning from his words. "On numerous occasions, the overly hasty interpretation of data has led to premature and unfounded conclusions that formed the basis for a degree of optimism or pessimism that ultimately proved largely unwarranted," he said.

"Please, let us proceed," said the Swiss banker. "Time is money."

"Unlike Time Warner," Rockefeller cracked.

Cheney looked at his watch. It was just a few minutes until the Appointment.

He cleared his throat. "The good news is I just saved the government a bundle by switching the insurance coverage on my armored vice-presidential limousine to Geico."

There was a general murmur of approval.

"The bad news is there is a very real danger that the existence of the Pact will soon become a matter of public record. Also, as of last October, the original Louisiana Purchase, an 828,000-square-mile chunk of our nation's heartland, comprising all or part of fifteen states with a total of 119 electoral votes, became, technically speaking, the property of the American Negro population of this country. In the 2000 election, we carried eleven of those states. The other four are key swing states. If we lose any of those electoral votes, we're toast."

The map of the 2000 results, with the Gore states in blue and the Bush states in red, was a real eye-opener. It looked as though someone had decided to highlight the Louisiana Purchase by coloring it in crimson ink.

"Oh, and by the way, most of the founding fathers were fags."

There was a sharp collective intake of breath.

Rumsfeld turned to Wolfowitz. "Why weren't you on top of this, Paul?" he demanded.

Wolfowitz turned to Feith. "Doug, how come you dropped the ball on this one?" he said.

Feith turned to Libby. "Scooter, I don't recall getting a heads-up on this from your office," he said.

Libby turned to Perle. "Wasn't this kind of thing in your bailiwick, Dick?" he inquired.

Perle put the tips of his fingers in the corners of his eyes and drew them into slits. "So solly," he said.

The UP arrow above the elevator door blinked on.

CHAPTER 27

SANDRA AND FRANKLIN emerged at street level from a narrow iron nineteenth-century coal chute door underneath the Capitol's central staircase. They quickly made their way through the wide plaza in front of the building and traversed 1st Street, heading toward the century-old Beaux Arts main building of the Library of Congress.

On their left was the Corinthian-columned white marble temple of the Supreme Court. A long line of reporters was waiting outside, hoping to get tickets to the morning session, where the justices were scheduled to hear arguments in *Krank v. Nutt,* a case whose outcome would determine whether the words "one nation, under God, armed, dangerous, and ready to kick some ass" would be added to the Pledge of Allegiance.

As the pair crossed East Capitol Street, they could see in the distance the handsome octagonal Greek Revival edifice housing the Drugstore of Congress, the elegant Georgian façade of the Dry Cleaners of Congress, and the elaborately turreted Romanesque-style brick superstructure of the Car Wash of Congress.

They passed the Library's flamboyant Neptune fountain, mounted the exuberantly ornamented staircase that graced the front of the masterpiece of academic French architecture, crossed the richly decorated entrance hall— now marred by the inevitable metal detectors—and made their way to the Research Center located at the edge of the spectacular domed hall that contained the Main Reading Room.

Sandra presented Senator Kydd's pass to the librarian on duty and gave him the catalog number. He entered it in a computer built into the reception desk. "There is no book listed under that number in the catalog of the Library of Congress," he stated unequivocally.

"That's impossible!" Sandra protested. "I know I got that number right. I read it out twice."

Franklin thought for a moment. "If there *were* a book with that number, where would I go to find it?" he asked.

The clerk tapped out a brief query on the computer's keyboard. "Stack G, level three," he said, pointing to a stairway that led to the subterranean repository housing the venerable institution's collection of 17 million books.

"What better place to hide a book than in a library that doesn't know it has it?" said Franklin as they descended into the building's basement storage area.

"You're right," Sandra agreed. "And they don't inspect people's bags for books they bring *in*—only for books they want to take out."

"Not only that, but Dumont didn't have to worry about someone coming along and deciding to borrow the book," Franklin added, adroitly plugging one of the few remaining holes in the noggin-numbing narrative's labyrinthine story line.

Three floors down, Sandra presented the card a second time at a jail-like barred door outside Stack G. A guard buzzed them in, and they entered a cement-walled room half the size of a football field. It was completely filled with rows of shelves, virtually every one of which was packed along its entire length with a section of the archive's six hundred miles of books.

The catalog prefixes were imprinted at the top of each rank of bookcases, and it took only a few minutes to locate the correct aisle. Franklin found the book about halfway down a row, on an upper shelf. He stood on tiptoes to reach it.

The number on its spine matched the number from the macaroni fastmail. He looked at the title: *The Big Book of Brain-teasers, Head-scratchers, and Mind-bogglers*. He groaned and handed it to Sandra.

Her face fell, but when she opened the book, her downcast expression was instantly replaced by a broad smile. The book was hollow, and in the shallow rectangular space left after half of its pages had been cut out, there was a thick color photograph with a grainy plastic surface.

It showed Hemmings Dumont sitting in a chair in a gallery in the Smithsonian. The picture was a hologram, and when Sandra held it up to the light, it showed a nearly three-dimensional view of the room.

Sandra turned it over. On the back was written a couplet:

> *An Arch atop this throne for years did perch;*
> *Beneath A Bunker is the place to search.*

"I'll take that, if you don't mind," said Howard Cheatham. He was holding a pistol.

"Oh, damn it to hell," said Sandra angrily. "He's the spy my uncle warned us about."

"A gun," Franklin exclaimed. "How did you get that in here?"

"It's plastic," said Sandra.

"Very observant, Miss Damsel," said Cheatham. "Actually, it's a water pistol, but it's not filled with ordinary water. It's filled with a saline solution containing a massive dose of Locust Valley Lockjaw Fever virus. Once it penetrates the skin—which it does very easily—you talk like Gloria Vanderbilt for about fifteen minutes, then you lapse into a permanent coma. Of course, if you live in Southampton or Palm Beach, nobody notices."

"Aren't you afraid of contracting it yourself?" Sandra asked. "You're not wearing any protection."

Cheatham smiled smugly. "I was vaccinated at Andover—everybody who goes to a decent private school gets shots for all the better diseases: Prep Throat, Old School Typhoid, Free-Range Chickenpox, Party-pooping Cough, Germantown Measles, Freshman Slumps, Button-down Cholera, Hookworm, Sliceworm, Twerpes, Plaid Cow, Loafer-and-Mouth, Boola-boolaremia, you name it."

"You're wasting your time," said Sandra. "I'm a C.D.C. officer—we get vaccinated for *everything*. Hell, I'm immune to Dutch Elm Disease."

Cheatham thought that over for a moment, then turned and pointed the pistol at Franklin. As he moved his arm, his jacket opened slightly and Franklin noticed the tiny gold pin in his tie.

"Skull and Bones," said Franklin.

Cheatham looked as if he had been slapped.

"I said, SKULL AND BONES!" said Franklin, practically shouting.

His face contorted in rage, Cheatham turned on his heel and left the room.

Sandra's jaw dropped. "It can't be that easy."

"Isn't it a little late in the game to be questioning preposterous plot twists?" Franklin asked crossly.

They made their way out of the stacks, up the stairs, and out through the huge bronze front doors.

"What's the quickest way to the Smithsonian?" Franklin wondered.

"Metro," said Sandra. "The Capitol South stop is three blocks from here."

They walked briskly down to the Metro entrance on 1st Street between C and D.

"Did you really get vaccinated for Locust Valley Fever?" Franklin asked Sandra as they hurried along.

"They had a vaccine, but I didn't take it—the potential side effects were too serious," said Sandra. "It can cause pre-senile dementia. First your memory starts becoming unreliable, then you begin to contradict yourself, and eventually you can't tell reality from make-believe." A note of dread crept into her voice. "I didn't want to end up like Condoleezza Rice."

On the escalator that led into the station, Sandra fished in her wallet and came up with a pair of valid fare cards. She kept one and gave the other to Franklin, and they went through the electronic turnstile and down another escalator, reaching the platform just as the row of softly flashing lights set into the pavement along its front edge started flashing, signaling the arrival of a westbound train.

"Ever notice how in thrillers the train always pulls into the station just as the characters get there?" asked Franklin.

"It's a nice perk," Sandra agreed, "but I'd rather have good medical and dental coverage and a shorter workday."

The subway's doors opened, and they entered the half-empty Orange Line train. They had been on the platform for only thirty seconds, but that was more than enough time for the security cameras mounted in hollows in the station's vaulted ceiling to record their images, and for the face-recognition software in the computers at the Department of Homeland Security to make a positive identification.

Sandra and Franklin sat down side by side on a bench-style seat. Sandra took out the picture and stared at it. Franklin looked over her shoulder.

They both figured it out at almost the same instant.

"Oh, Archie," said Sandra.

"Oh, Edith," said Franklin.

The doors closed and the train whooshed out of the station.

CHAPTER 28

THE LIGHT ABOVE the elevator in the inner conference room at the Presidential Emergency Operations Center under the White House blinked off, a bell dinged, and the doors opened. The cabin was filled with a thick, yellowish haze, and there was a distinct odor of sulfur. A figure stepped forward out of the mist.

It was Richard Nixon.

He looked fabulous. His face was lightly tanned, he had lost some weight, and his blue suit, for once, seemed to fit.

"Let me just say how glad I am to be here again," he said.

Queen Elizabeth's corgi barked sharply, and except for England's dowdy monarch, everyone started to rise to their feet, but Nixon signaled them to sit back down.

"No, no need for that," he said, taking his seat at the head of the table facing Cheney. "I'm just an ordinary citizen now, a mere mortal." He caught himself. "Well, a former mortal," he said, laughing in his customary labored fashion. He nodded to his former colleagues, Cheney, Rumsfeld, and Kissinger. "Dick, Don, Henry—long time no see."

"Sir, you look terrific, if I may say so," said Rumsfeld. "They must be treating you well, um, down there."

"Can't complain," said Nixon. "It's a lot like Los Angeles, but without the traffic problems. You can build a lot of freeways if you don't have any do-gooders around to stand in your way," he said, winking conspiratorially.

Nixon looked around the room. "You know, the last time I was down here—I suppose I should say *up* here—was just before I left office. Henry, you remember that meeting, don't you?" he said, looking at Kissinger.

"Yes, Mr. President, it vas a most notevorthy evening."

"I was trying to come up with some way to stay in office—you know, cook up some crisis, declare martial law, postpone elections," he said, "and guess who came through that door?" He gestured awkwardly over his shoulder at the elevator.

"Lyndon Johnson." Nixon smiled. "And you know what he said to me?" He paused for effect. "He said, 'Nixon, do you really want to go down in history as a bigger asshole than me?' " Nixon shook his head in wonderment at the recollection.

Cheney looked sick.

Nixon fixed the row of Bush administration officials with an icy stare. His tone changed abruptly.

"You're a bunch of goddamn clowns," he said sharply. "What have you been smoking? You invaded a country that isn't tiny, and isn't nearby, and isn't filled with Spanish-speaking people. You've let those wacko Bible-thumpers hijack the Republican Party. You've managed to make the Democrats look like models of fiscal responsibility. You've pissed off the Europeans, who are the only people on the goddamn globe who don't want to slit our throats. And to top it all off, you all went and spilled your guts to that no-good son of a bitch *Bob Woodward!*" Nixon was practically shouting, and his face was contorted with rage.

A whistling sound emanated from inside his jacket pocket, and he reached in and took out a six-inch-high, red-skinned devil with horns, a tail, and a little pitchfork. He placed the diminutive demon on his left shoulder, and it leaned over and whispered in his ear. Nixon nodded, put the tiny goblin back in his pocket, and got up.

"The Boss has decided—we're throwing our support to Senator Kerry," he said, and walked to the elevator. Queen Elizabeth's corgi let out a howl and came running over, nipping at Nixon's ankles. Displaying a grace he had rarely possessed in life, he gave the diminutive dog a perfectly executed kick that sent it flying across the room. He smiled broadly, and as the elevator doors opened, he stepped in, then turned around and raised his arm. As the mist rose around him and the doors slowly closed, he repeated the famous farewell wave he had given as he boarded the helicopter following his resignation.

Cheney looked down the left side of the table. Rockefeller and Greenspan were already sporting Kerry buttons. Murdoch had replaced the American flag in his lapel with a tiny Australian emblem. The Swiss banker was methodically tearing up a campaign contribution check into smaller and smaller pieces. Henry Kissinger had pulled over a large glass ashtray and was busily burning a small trove of incriminating documents in a tidy little bonfire. Queen Elizabeth comforted her stunned corgi and began drafting a royal decree conferring on Senator John F. Kerry the title of Right Honourable Freeloader of the British Empire, with Full Access to the Fridge.

CHAPTER 29

SANDRA AND FRANKLIN exited from the north end of the Smithsonian Metro station and walked straight across the Mall to the National Museum of American History. A school bus was parked outside on Madison Drive, and as they went in the museum's Mall-side entrance, children began noisily pouring out of the battered yellow vehicle.

Franklin followed Sandra through the nearly empty galleries. She stopped at the American Encounters exhibit. There, on its own raised and roped-off platform, stood Archie Bunker's chair.

"An Arch atop this throne for years did perch," Franklin recited.

"Beneath A Bunker is the place to search," said Sandra, completing the couplet.

They waited a moment for a bored guard to wander off, then they ran onto the platform, lifted up the seat cushion, and began probing deep in the gaps in the chair's inner upholstery. Sandra found it almost immediately. It was a little brass telescope.

She shook it. There was something inside. She tried unscrewing the eyepiece, but it was part of the metal cylinder. She tried the lens on the front, and it came off easily. A small sheet of rolled-up paper fell out.

She read its contents aloud.

Oh that man from Monticello
was a most far-seeing fellow;
you'll see why our peeping Thomas
chose this site to keep his promise.

"Gaaaaaah!" she cried in frustration. "I've had it with this gobbledygook!"

At that moment, the guard came back in the room. "Sorry, folks," he said amiably, "but I'll have to ask you not to touch the exhibits."

They stepped down quickly from the platform. "See

you got the copy of Jefferson's telescope from the gift shop," he said. "Got one for my kid."

Sandra and Franklin exchanged glances.

"Science in Colonial American Life, first floor," said Sandra, and they raced down the stairs.

Not including the tripod, the telescope was about three feet long and made of shiny brass. It sat by itself in the corner of a room filled with eighteenth-century scientific instruments: surveying equipment, a barometer, several nautical chronometers, a variety of sextants, and an original Franklin lightning rod.

The only other people in the room were an older couple who left just as Sandra and Franklin walked in. Sandra went directly over to the telescope and peered through the front lens, but the way the glass had been ground made it nearly opaque from the outside. She tried unscrewing the lens, but it wouldn't budge. Franklin took it off its tripod and wedged it between his legs. He gave it a try; after a couple of false starts, the cap finally began to turn easily, and he twisted it all the way off.

He handed the telescope to Sandra. She took a deep breath, then looked inside. The parchments were rolled up inside the antique spyglass. The sealed two-and-a-half-inch-diameter tube had provided a perfect storage compartment. Because of the way the simple optics worked, the telescope was still perfectly functional, even with its interior lined with documents, and its contents were invisible to anyone looking through the device from either end.

Sandra handed the telescope back to Franklin and took out her cell phone. Franklin unbuckled his belt and slipped the telescope tube into his right trouser leg.

She hesitated for a moment. "We need to talk to Senator Kydd, but I'm sure this call will be intercepted."

"I'll speak to him in Latin," said Franklin. She punched in the senator's private office number, and Kydd came right on the line. Sandra gave Franklin the phone.

"*Ave, senator,*" said Franklin. "*Litteras repperimus.*" We found the documents.

"*Tibi eas ferimus.*" We're bringing them to you.

"*Adiutor tuus proditor est.*" Your aide is a traitor.

"*Sic, Senator. Salve,*" said Franklin, closing the phone and handing it back to Sandra.

"What did he say?"

" '*Hilda pediculum castigabit*' and '*Cave culos,*' " said Franklin. " 'Hilda will take care of, um, Howie,' and 'Beware of, er, bad people.' "

* * *

"Excuse me, could you direct me to the office of the curator?" said a pleasant voice behind them.

Sandra and Franklin were equally startled. Sandra almost dropped her phone, and Franklin nearly fell over. He finished fastening his pants.

"I'm sorry if I'm interrupting anything," said Quick Brown Fox. He opened his satchel and took out the medicine stick. "I have some Indian artifacts I want to place in the custody of a government official."

"Well, *I'm* a government official," said Attorney General John Ashcroft, entering the room at the head of a small team of F.B.I. agents. Two of them had their guns drawn.

"Now, I do recognize Professor Franklin and Agent Sandra Damsel from their photographs, but who might you be, and what is in that bag?" he demanded of Quick Brown Fox.

"My name is Ben Fox," he replied. "I'm here on tribal business."

"How!" said Ashcroft, holding up his palm in a tactless parody of an Indian greeting. He motioned to two agents, who grabbed the bag away from Fox.

One looked inside. "Just an old skull," he said.

Fox's eyes flashed. "It is the skull of the great warrior Geronimo. I am returning it to his people."

"Woo woo woo," said Ashcroft, waving his hand toward his mouth and making a mocking Indian war call.

Fox looked at the agents and weighed his chances of killing them all. Ashcroft saw the menace in his eyes.

"Heap big chief will be in heap big trouble if him decide to go on warpath," said Ashcroft.

Fox slowly raised the medicine stick and began to chant. He wasn't sure he remembered all the words of the appeal to the Spirits of the Sky, but it really didn't matter, because the rainmaking power imparted to the talisman by one of the greatest shamans of the western Plains was so great, it wouldn't have mattered if he had sung the theme from *Gilligan's Island*.

"Hey-yah hey-yah hey-yah hey," he cried, and with a series of sharp *pling*s the sprinkler heads in the gallery ceiling went off one after the other in rapid succession, and a phenomenal volume of water poured down on the room's flabbergasted occupants.

The sudden pressure drop in the museum's fire suppression system automatically cut electrical power to the entire floor, and the windowless exhibition area was plunged into darkness.

Sandra grabbed Franklin's arm. "Quick," she hissed into his ear, "I know the way." She pulled him through an exit, and he hobbled behind her, the telescope hampering his movements. Relying on memories of the building's lay-out from countless visits to the museum to see her uncle, she navigated through the pitch-dark, but thankfully dry, corridors.

They could still hear the Indian chanting and Ashcroft shouting for someone to bring a light as Sandra suddenly stopped in front of an exhibit that was feebly lit by the red-dish glow of an emergency exit sign.

"That's the only way out," she said.

"Oh, no," he protested.

"Oh, yes," she insisted.

CHAPTER 30

THE BUSLOAD OF students was bitterly disappointed when the overwhelmed but good-natured substitute teacher who was leading the class's expedition informed them that the school visit to the Smithsonian had to be canceled because of a malfunction in a sprinkler system, but their cranky mood quickly turned to joy when they saw who—or what—was lurching down the short flight of steps from the museum's entrance.

"Look," one of the children cried as Sandra and Franklin made their way unsteadily down the stairs in the heavy, two-person Muppet outfit. "It's Snuffleupagus!"

"Not so fast, Shag Pile," an F.B.I. agent on guard duty

outside ordered peremptorily. "You're not going any-where."

Sandra, who occupied the front half of the bulky costume, turned in his direction. "We—I mean I—am part of the President's No Child Left Behind initiative," she declared in a high-pitched, singsongy voice. "George Bush takes education very seriously. How would you like to spend the next couple of years giving parking tickets to car bombers in Baghdad?" she asked, her voice filled with un-Muppet-like menace.

The agent backed off. "OK, you can go," he said, "but no funny stuff."

The children cheered. Sandra started walking toward the school bus, and Franklin, bending forward uncomfortably in the rear segment of the clumsy getup, did his best to mimic her movements. She leaned over to the teacher. "Excuse me, Mr. Teacher, but do you think you could give us a ride in your bussy-wussy up to the Capitol? I'm scheduled to testify before the Foreign Relations Committee on behalf of puppet governments everywhere," she said, winging it wildly.

"Well," said the teacher agreeably, "that would give us something to do, and provide the children with an opportunity to see how our government works."

"You want to show them how our government works,

take them to the zoo, go to the Reptile House," said a sour voice from deep inside Snuffy's furry torso.

Sandra kicked Franklin in the shin. "Ow," he said.

"I thought Snuffy never talked," one fat little boy complained.

"Normally, I don't," said Sandra in her extremely unconvincing falsetto, "but I'm learning how so I can audition for *The Apprentice*."

Sandra waited until all the children had reboarded the bus, then she and Franklin waddled up its stairs and positioned themselves in the aisle.

The bus pulled away from the curb and headed along the Mall toward the Capitol.

The Department of Homeland Security surveillance analyst passed the printout of the cell-phone intercept to the chief linguistics officer.

"What do you make of this?" he asked.

"Looks like Latin," said the expert. "Give it to the Latin American desk."

The analyst took it and placed it in the in-box of the Southern Hemisphere specialist, who was busy installing tiny bugging devices in a pair of castanets. He didn't look up from his work.

---

* * *

The school bus turned off Constitution Avenue and entered the curving approach road that led to the front of the Senate Wing of the Capitol. It parked near the main stairs, and Sandra and Franklin, still in the Snuffleupagus suit, clomped out of the bus. The children happily piled out after them.

At the foot of the steps, looking stern, were the top two congressional protocol officers, the sergeant-at-arms and standing next to him, his hands on his hips and his elbows bent forward defiantly, the sergeant-at-arms-akimbo.

Behind them, a pair of medical orderlies was helping Cheatham down the stairs. The bandage on his head and the temporary sling that supported his right arm were clear signs that when the senator had told Hilda to give Howie the heave-ho, she had carried out his instructions with literal-minded gusto. He would be in for some awkward moments in the emergency room when the attending physicians tried to discuss with him the injuries to his skull and bones.

Senator Kydd himself stood at the top of the stairs, looking anxiously for any sign of the intrepid pair of patriots on whose shoulders rested the future of the country.

Sandra towed Franklin forward, and they approached the sergeant-at-arms. Sandra leaned over to the startled officer and spoke to him urgently. He immediately ran up the stairs and conferred briefly with Kydd. The senator smiled broadly.

"*Ave,* Snuffleupagus!" he called out.

They had made it.

EPILOGUE

THE TWO-HUNDRED-YEAR-OLD parchments, their edges held down by a scattering of books, lay flat on a spacious conference table next to the empty telescope. Kydd was mesmerized by the astonishing sheaf of documents.

The intercom buzzed. "Senator, Bob Woodward is on his way over from *The Washington Post,* Mike Wallace will be here at noon with a film crew from *60 Minutes,* and I have David Boies on the line."

Kydd picked up the phone. It was always a pleasure to speak with the distinguished attorney who had argued *Bush v. Gore* before the Supreme Court.

"Mr. Boies," said Kydd, "how would you like to represent thirty-five million plaintiffs in a ten-trillion-dollar property rights case and, in the process, obtain some small measure of sweet revenge over those scoundrels who stole the 2000 presidential election?"

Sandra and Franklin stood together on the senator's terrace, admiring the spectacular view of the Mall. Visible in the distance was the boxy limestone structure of the National Museum of American History.

"It's hard to believe this whole thing started right down there only twelve hours ago," said Franklin. He had inadvertently rested his palm on a dab of pigeon doo on the stone balustrade of the grand balcony, and as he abruptly snatched his hand off the slimy spot, he noticed something odd. His signet ring had swiveled open. He remembered banging the thing against the telescope when he was extricating himself from the Muppet outfit.

"My ring!" he exclaimed. "It's got a secret compartment!"

"Nooooooooo!" Sandra wailed.

"Wait," said Franklin, peering into the pellet-size recess. "It's empty!"

"No message in tiny type?" Sandra demanded. "No

teensy-weensy radio? No itsy-bitsy computer chip? No microdot? No nanobot? No subplot?"

"Nothing," said Franklin. They both breathed deep sighs of relief.

"You know," he said softly, "I won't miss wrestling with stupid puzzles or dodging poison darts, but I am going to miss you."

Sandra smiled and looked into his eyes. "Ever notice how in thrillers, right at the very end, the relationship between the heroine and the hero, which up until that point has remained formal and businesslike, suddenly deepens into something far more intimate, and the bond they steadily developed as they faced danger together all at once blossoms into love?"

Their lips met in a passionate kiss, and as they embraced, the last of the long, description-laden sentences trailed off across the page toward the final punctuation mark, and there was nothing left but an empty, snow-white expanse of blissfully blank paper.

A Note on the Type

The text of this book was set in Balderdash, a highly embellished barefaced font ideally suited for pulp fiction. Eye-catching and easy to skim, it was originally designed in 1789 by Thomas Buncombe for use in a series of cheaply printed handbills promoting real estate investments on the continent of Atlantis. It is unique in the history of typography for having the minutest fine print ever produced, a completely illegible 1-point condensed version that can be read only through a high-powered microscope.

ABOUT THE AUTHOR

HENRY BEARD attended Harvard College and was a member of the *Harvard Lampoon* during the period when it published nationally noted parodies of *Playboy, Life,* and *Time*. He went on to found the *National Lampoon* with Douglas Kenney (the writer-producer of *Animal House* and *Caddyshack*) and served as its editor during the magazine's heyday in the 1970s. He is the author or coauthor of five *New York Times* bestsellers—*Miss Piggy's Guide to Life; Sailing: A Sailor's Dictionary; French for Cats; Leslie Nielsen's Stupid Little Golf Book;* and *O.J.'s Legal Pad*—and more than two dozen other popular humorous works, including *Latin for All Occasions, Xtreme Latin, Bill Gates' Super Secret Laptop, The Official Politically Correct Dictionary, Zen for Cats, Mulligan's Laws,* and a series of humorous pocket dictionaries, including *Golfing, Fishing, Skiing,* and *Sailing*.